BY WILLIAM SAFIRE AND LEONARD SAFIR

Good Advice on Writing
Leadership
Words of Wisdom: More Good Advice
Good Advice

BY WILLIAM SAFIRE

LANGUAGE

Coming to Terms
Fumblerules
Language Maven Strikes Again
You Could Look It Up
Take My Word for It
I Stand Corrected: More on Language
What's the Good Word?
On Language

POLITICS

Safire's Washington
Before the Fall
Safire's Political Dictionary
Plunging Into Politics
The Relations Explosion

FICTION

Freedom
Full Disclosure

GOOD ADVICE
ON WRITING

WRITERS PAST AND PRESENT ON HOW TO WRITE WELL

Compiled and Edited by
WILLIAM SAFIRE
and
LEONARD SAFIR

SIMON & SCHUSTER
New York   London   Toronto   Sydney   Tokyo   Singapore

SIMON & SCHUSTER
Simon & Schuster Building
Rockefeller Center
1230 Avenue of the Americas
New York, New York 10020

Designed by Irving Perkins Associates
Manufactured in the United States of America

1   3   5   7   9   10   8   6   4   2

Library of Congress Cataloging-in-Publication Data

Good advice on writing : writers past and present on how to write well
/ compiled and edited by William Safire and Leonard Safir.
p.   cm.
Includes bibliographical references and index.
ISBN: 0-671-77005-5
1. Authorship—Quotations, maxims, etc.   2. Authors—Quotations.
I. Safire, William, date   .   II. Safir, Leonard, date
PN165.G66   1992   92–19222
808'.02—dc20   CIP

To
Aunt Pearl and Aunt "Toots" (Dorothy)

CONTENTS

A
Preface
Quotation

Ah, ye knights of the pen! May honour be your shield,
and truth tip your lances! Be gentle to all gentle
people. Be modest to women. Be tender to children.
And as for the Ogre Humbug, out sword and have at him!

—William Makepeace Thackeray

PREFACE

ON READING LIKE A WRITER

By William Safire

At the first meeting in 1967 plotting a presidential campaign, Richard Nixon introduced me to the half-dozen political conspirators in the Herbert Hoover Suite of New York's Waldorf-Astoria with these words: "This is Safire, absolutely trustworthy, worked with us in '60. But," that untrusting soul added, "watch what you say, he's a writer."

In retrospect, I take it as a compliment; a writer is a fine thing to be, and not one writer working in the White House has ever been indicted. In the years since, I have come to fancy myself as Hydra, the Greek water monster with nine heads that grew back two heads for every one cut off; mine have included reporter, press agent, lexicographer, speechwriter, novelist, pundit, anthologist, language maven—that's close enough to nine—with each head certain of itself as a writer. (Go ahead, chop off my novelist's head: I'll grow you the noggins of a playwright and a political theologist.) All these sometimes confused heads have the god of communication's uncommon denominator: Many of us have been in varying lines of work, but insist that first and last we are writers.

That's because writing is less a profession than a professing—a way of stimulating, organizing, and affirming thoughts to give meaning to some slice of life. When you're tired of writing, you're tired of life. (Did Samuel Johnson say something similar about London? Worry not about plagiarism; with an oblique reference, a new dictum can stand on an old aphorism's shoulders.)

There; after a catchy anecdotal lede, I have presented my cre-

11

dentials, targeted my audience, and—having selected a breezily didactic tone—am now prepared to state the purpose of this preface. The trusting reader will assume this to be teaching by example, the lesson being: The writer should determine his audience, adopt a style and tone to fit it, and then make the point.

Don't fall for it. That pedantry is for hand-wringing hacks. Writers are not in the business of marketing; they have chosen the world of invention. To write creatively is to come up with something new or at least to come at something differently. Whether in arranging fact or hatching fiction, originality is inner-directed, not audience-driven.

This anthology is for the reading writer; specifically, the writer interested in good advice from successful practitioners in the art of transmitting original ideas. Although you are at the moment in the role of a reader, I presume you are a writer, or would like to be a writer, or get a kick out of hanging around writers and would not be averse to having them consider you a valuable associate. For me—the one doing the writing in this writer-reader symbiosis— that happily defines this book's primary audience, but to you—the newly warned reading writer—it should raise the question: Is it a good idea for a writer to try to define an audience? More broadly, whom is the writer writing for? (When "whom" is correct, recast the sentence.) What audience are you aiming at? William Zinsser, quoted herein, has this answer: "You are writing for yourself. . . . Don't try to guess what sort of thing editors want to publish or what you think the country is in a mood to read. Editors and readers don't know what they want to read until they read it."

Writing for yourself is not as arrogant as it seems. Of course, style should befit the occasion—you don't wear black tie to a picnic—and no integrity is lost by taking different tones, or even choosing different subjects, in addressing the garden club, the political convention, or the professional society. But in the big writing decisions, from the selection of theme to the evocation of character, the good writer thinks only of an audience of Number One. Self-indulgent? Sure; that's one of the pleasures that come with the pain of pulling a real purpose out of your mind. Creative authenticity comes from seeking to suit oneself and rarely springs from a desire to please others.

Journalists, who think of their writing as a craft more than an art, have this criterion in judging the worth of an investigative piece: Does it advance the story? An editor can immediately tell the difference between a classy rehash and an article that does its heavy lifting toward the revelation of some truth. E. B. White called such "ascent" the heart of the writing matter, and derided the would-be writers who thought their audience might not be ready for the climb: "A writer who questions the capacity of the person at the other end of the line is not a writer at all, merely a schemer." In a more profound way, that necessity for ascent or advancement applies to writing as art: "The artist must raise everything to a higher level," wrote Flaubert. "He is like a pump; inside him is a great pipe reaching down into the bowels of things, the deepest layers. He sucks up what was pooled beneath the surface and brings it forth into the sunlight in giant sprays."

Let such a simile be your umbrella when considering the advice collected mainly by my brother Len, the full-time anthologist, with some help from me. As you dip into the insights and outrages herein about every facet of composition, remember this caveat: Nobody who intends to be a writer can afford to be an unwary or passive reader. A moment ago, I crossed you up with a "Don't fall for it"; that was intended to be jarring, to raise suspicion, to induce the reading writer to read less like a reader and more like a writer.

When writers read, they read with narrowed eyes, knowing that their emotions or thought processes are being manipulated and subtly directed by a fellow member of the scribe tribe. Writers read skeptically, often doubtfully, sometimes combatively; they take an active part in a textual exchange, inwardly commenting "Good," or "Wrong," or "Why?" and lubricating or challenging the prose by mentally larding in personal experience in support or refutation. Reading writers are never mere receptacles.

On the contrary, reading writers understand they are objects of another writer's purpose, whether in a long passage or brief aphorism. As they discern it, they may resist or cooperate, but cannot remain uninvolved so long as the writer is not merely amusing or prostituting himself. "Let every man take care how he talks, or how he writes of other men," wrote Cervantes, "and not set down at random, higgle-de-piggledy, whatever comes into his noddle." Both reading writer and writing writer know that purpose is all: Be funny when you can, but always be serious about your aim.

Read the sometimes conflicting advice of other writers to help

13

sharpen that purpose, but read with those narrowed eyes. (That's why so many writers squint; it's not bad lighting but inculcated skepticism.) See how a point about composition can be made with metaphor, but don't fall in love with the point because of the aptness of the figure of speech. "A sentence should read," wrote Thoreau, "as if its author, had he held a plough instead of a pen, could have drawn a furrow deep and straight to the end." Ah, that's good—but what of the sentence that curves around and bites the unsuspecting reader in the backside? Nothing could be more boring than great fields of straight furrows. Raymond Chandler was more practical: "When the plot flags, bring in a man with a gun." But that may be too practical; Somerset Maugham had some astringent advice for seekers of mechanistic counsel: "There are three rules for writing the novel. Unfortunately, no one knows what they are."

There are rules for writing clear English prose, too, and some of us claim to know what they are, but the reading writer is not intimidated by advice on grammar. It helps to know what a gerund is, and to understand syntax so that you can plow your furrow as you furrow your brow; it helps even more to know the etymons of words, thereby to paint prose in the color of connotation. But the technique of writing is not what you can best glean from the advice herein. "Technique holds a reader from sentence to sentence," writes Joyce Carol Oates, "but only content will stay in his mind."

Content is determined by a writer's purpose, focus, and guts. Faulkner had it right: "A writer must teach himself that the basest of all things is to be afraid." Melville said it better: "I love all men who *dive*. Any fish can swim near the surface, but it takes a great whale to go downstairs five miles or more." He likened such plunging to writers who recklessly went deep for ideas, hailing "that whole corps of thought-divers, that have been diving and coming up again with bloodshot eyes since the world began."

The reading writer will acknowledge the force in that "with bloodshot eyes" but wonder if this introduction is too studded with quotations. Of course it would be, for any piece of writing other than a prolegomenon for an anthology of writing advice; in this case, however, quotation frenzy is not only suitable, but required. Sometimes the eye too narrowed on technique misses the point of purpose and content.

When it comes to writers and writing, "being a writer," wallowing in what we are, is all too often a pose, an affectation of some romantic if not lucrative lifestyle. Being what you are—the reading writer—is not nearly as important as doing what you should do: advancing the story, raising whatever you touch to a higher level, expressing ideas in new ways that illuminate or inspire, inducing the world to watch what you say; in a word (specifically, a gerund), writing.

A

ACCURACY

Let every man take care how he talks, or how he writes of other men, and not set down at random, higgle-de-piggledy, whatever comes into his noddle.

—CERVANTES

Nothing is sillier than the creative writing teacher's dictum "Write about what you know." But whether you're writing about people or dragons, your personal observation of how things happen in the world—how character reveals itself—can turn a dead scene into a vital one. Preliminary good advice might be: Write as if you were a movie camera. Get exactly what is there. . . . The trick is to bring it out, get it down. Getting it down precisely is all that is meant by "the accuracy of the writer's eye." Getting down what the writer really cares about—setting down what the writer himself notices, as opposed to what any fool might notice—is all that is meant by the *originality* of the writer's eye. Every human being has original vision. Most can't write it down without cheapening or falsifying.

—JOHN GARDNER

One should always aim at being interesting, rather than exact.

—Voltaire

(*See Clarity, Details, Precision.*)

ACTION

One evening in March, 1873, he (Tolstoy) found a volume of tales by Pushkin in the living room and began reading passages aloud to his wife. He was struck by the opening sentence of one tale: "The guests arrived at the country house." "That's the way for us to write," he exclaimed to Sonja. "Anyone else would start by describing the guests, the rooms, but he jumps straight into the action." Later that same evening, Tolstoy went to his study and started *Anna Karenina*.

—Malcolm Cowley

(*See Beginning, Openings.*)

ADJECTIVES

As to the adjective: when in doubt, strike it out.

—Mark Twain

Generally use transitive verbs, that strike their object; and use them in the active voice, eschewing the stationary passive, with its little auxiliary is's and was's, and its participles getting into the light of your adjectives, which should be few. For, as rough law, by his use of the straight, by his economy of adjectives, you can tell a man's style, if it be masculine or neuter, writing or "composition."

—Arthur Quiller-Couch

Go easy on the adjectives and adverbs because in most cases two adjectives for one noun compete with each other for the reader's fullest response and both tend to lose; adverbs modifying verbs tend also to dilute the impact of the verb: " 'Die!' he shouted insanely." The word "die," with its exclamation point, is already too much, "shouted" is implied, and "insanely" overwhelms all three words before it. The effort collapses under its competing components.

—DAVID MADDEN

ADVERBS

The colorless verb needs to be looked to in nearly all amateur writing. It can, of course, be over-colored. J. J. Montague's burlesque of contemporary stylistic prose—" 'Don't kiss me,' she insincered. 'Why not?' he curioused. 'Because—' she uneasied."—is both a warning and a guide. The conspicuous use of verbs in which adverbs are implicit is unfortunate, as in any conspicuous struggle for effect, but "she said insincerely," "he asked curiously," "she answered uneasily" makes quite as hard reading.

—EDITH RONALD MIRRIELEES

Nouns, verbs, are the workhorses of the language. Especially in dialogue, don't say, "she said mincingly," or "he said boisterously." Just say, "he said, she said."

—JOHN P. MARQUAND

A really civilized and cultivated writer of the English language will turn inside out to avoid adverbs. When you're young, you don't realize that's a lazy way of characterizing what someone says— "she said sadly," "gaily," "bitterly," "coldly." You shouldn't do it.

—MARCIA DAVENPORT

(See Verbs.)

AFFECTATION

Look for all *fancy* wordings and get rid of them. . . . Avoid all terms and expressions, old or new, that embody affectation. Why *dual zone refrigerators, dual biography, dual (traffic) lane*? Why *dialogue* in every context, including negotiations at a distance between whole nations? Why the sign near a private beach: Beware! Dog is *Carnivorous*? Why, in the White House, a *cosmic* review of economic policy?

—JACQUES BARZUN

AIM

It is his [the poet's, the writer's] privilege to help man endure by lifting his heart, by reminding him of the courage and honor and hope and pride and compassion and pity and sacrifice which have been the glory of his past. The poet's voice need not merely be the record of man, it can be one of the props, the pillars to help him endure and prevail.

—WILLIAM FAULKNER, speech
upon receiving the Nobel Prize,
1950

My task which I am trying to achieve is, by the power of the written word to make you hear, to make you feel—it is, before all, to make you see. That—and no more, and it is everything.

—JOSEPH CONRAD

If a writer were a free man and not a slave, if he could write what he chose, not what he must, if he could base his work upon his own feeling and not upon convention, there would be no plot, no comedy, no tragedy, no love interest or catastrophe in the accepted style, and perhaps not a single button sewn on as the Bond Street tailors would have it. Life is not a series of giglamps symmetrically arranged; but a luminous halo, a semitransparent envelope surrounding us from the beginning of consciousness to the end. Is it not the task of the novelist to convey this varying, this unknown and uncircumscribed spirit, whatever aberration of complexity it may display, with as little mixture of the alien and external as possible?

—Virginia Woolf

To live, to err, to fall, to triumph, to recreate life out of life! . . . On and on and on and on!

—James Joyce

If the question is "Should one aim high?" the answer is "Yes." Not every writer has it in him to write "the great American novel." The trick is to do your best. It is an unfortunate fact of life that too many writers—like too many people in other fields—are satisfied with less than their best.

—Sidney Sheldon

The only end of writing is to enable the reader better to enjoy life, or better to endure it.

—Samuel Johnson

I've always tried to write for the long run.

—James T. Farrell

The aim, if reached or not, makes great the life;
Try to be Shakespeare, leave the rest to fate.

—ROBERT BROWNING

(See Challenge, Purpose.)

AMBIGUITY

No word or phrase should be ambiguous.

The disastrous charge of the Light Brigade at Balaclava in the Crimean War was made because of a carelessly worded order to "charge for the guns"—meaning that some British guns which were in an exposed position should be hauled out of reach of the enemy, not that the Russian batteries should be charged. But even in the calmest times it is often very difficult to compose an English sentence that cannot possibly be misunderstood.

—ROBERT GRAVES and ALAN
HODGE

AMBITION TO WRITE

To sum it all up, if you want to write, if you want to create, you must be the most sublime fool that God ever turned out and sent rambling.

You must write every single day of your life.

You must read dreadful dumb books and glorious books, and let them wrestle in beautiful fights inside your head, vulgar one moment, brilliant the next.

You must lurk in libraries and climb the stacks like ladders to sniff books like perfumes and wear books like hats upon your crazy heads.

I wish for you a wrestling match with your Creative Muse that will last a lifetime.

I wish craziness and foolishness and madness upon you.

May you live with hysteria, and out of it make fine stories—science fiction or otherwise.

Which finally means, may you be in love every day for the next 20,000 days. And out of that love, remake a world.

—RAY BRADBURY

(*See Aim, Pride in Being a Writer, Purpose, Self-Revelation.*)

APPROACHES

She says she approaches her writing "sideways, like a horse, starting by writing letters or something and then creeping up on a novel."

—MARY WESLEY

Write in any way that works for you. Write in a tuxedo or in the shower with a raincoat or in a cave deep in the woods.

—JOHN GARDNER

I do most of my work sitting down. That's where I shine.

—ROBERT BENCHLEY

(*See Attitude, Maturation, Urgency.*)

ARTISTRY

A work that aspires, however humbly, to the condition of art, should carry its justification in every line.

—JOSEPH CONRAD

The first art work in an artist is the shaping of his own personality.

—NORMAN MAILER

I think that someone who pretends to be a storyteller has to be a prophet, clown, trickster, and magician. A creative person—let's say that awful word: an artist—makes what we call magical operations. Because if something lives only in his imagination, totally hidden to others, then people won't be able to imagine it. So, with his talent, experience, artisanal sense, materials and colors, an artist makes things visible for everybody, like the magician in a fairy tale who makes something that wasn't there suddenly appear. Because the artist always lives somewhere in between the unconscious and the prevailing cultural standards, and he attempts to combine the two.

—FEDERICO FELLINI

True ease in writing comes from art, not chance.
As those move easiest who have learn'd to dance.
'Tis not enough no harshness gives offense,
The sound must seem an echo to the sense.

—ALEXANDER POPE

(See Craftsmanship, Professionalism.)

ATTITUDE

There are no good stories. Only the singer really matters, seldom the song. What a writer brings to any story is an attitude, an attitude usually defined by the wound stripes of life.

—JOHN GREGORY DUNNE

Technique and verbal resources are indispensable, but writing can not be mechanized. It is a mode of action, and as with all action, its quality is ultimately determined by the attitude from which it springs. Quite simply, the writer must feel his responsibilities: responsibility to protect the trust on which all communication depends; responsibility to himself, to make what he says declare his mind; responsibility to his subject, to deliver it whole and unmarred; responsibility to the language, to keep our most precious cultural possession clean and ready for use.

—WILLIAM R. KEAST and ROBERT
E. STREETER

No matter how piercing and appalling his insights, the desolation creeping over his outer world, the lurid lights and shadows of his inner world, the writer must live with hope, work in faith.

—J. B. PRIESTLEY

The artist must raise everything to a higher level: he is like a pump; inside him is a great pipe reaching down into the bowels of things, the deepest layers. He sucks up what was pooled beneath the surface and brings it forth into the sunlight in giant sprays.

—GUSTAVE FLAUBERT

My attitude has never changed. I cannot imagine feeling lackadaisical about a performance. I treat each encounter as a matter of life and death. The one important thing I have learned over the years is the difference between taking one's work seriously and taking one's self seriously. The first is imperative and the second disastrous.

—MARGOT FONTEYN

(*See Approaches, Maturation, Tone.*)

AUDIENCE

An author ought to write for the youth of his generation, the critics of the next, and the schoolmasters of ever afterwards.

—F. Scott Fitzgerald

"Who am I writing for?" It's a fundamental question and it has a fundamental answer: You are writing for yourself. Don't try to visualize the great mass audience. There is no such audience— every reader is a different person. Don't try to guess what sort of thing editors want to publish or what you think the country is in a mood to read. Editors and readers don't know what they want to read until they read it. Besides, they're always looking for something new.

—William Zinsser

Even before he sharpens his pencil, the expository writer must ask himself four questions: What specific point do I intend to make? Is it worth making? For whom am I writing? How can I best convey my point to my readers? Unless the writer has carefully answered each of these questions no amount of good grammar and correct spelling will save him, and his composition is already worthless even before he begins to scribble. Deciding upon reader and purpose is easily half the task of writing. . . . The first requirement of all writing—a definite point for definite readers.

—Thomas S. Kane and Leonard
J. Peters

Write about *real things,* for God's sake: blondes and pistons!

—Young teacher quoted by
James Merrill

Your audience is one single reader. I have found that sometimes it helps to pick out one person—a real person you know, or an imagined person, and write to that one.

—John Steinbeck

Writing is one of the few professions left where you take all the responsibility for what you do. It's really dangerous and ultimately destroys you as a writer if you start thinking about responses to your work or what your audience needs.

—Erica Jong

The first essential is to know what one wishes to say; the second is to decide to whom one wishes to say it.

—Harold Nicolson

Better to write for yourself and have no public, than write for the public and have no self.

—Cyril Connolly

The whole duty of a writer is to please and satisfy himself, and the true writer always plays to an audience of one.

—E. B. White

AUTOBIOGRAPHY

When writing of oneself one should show no mercy. Yet why—at the first attempt to discover one's own truth—does all inner strength seem to melt away in floods of self-pity and tenderness and rising tears?

—GEORGES BERNANOS

You have to take pains in a memoir not to hang on the reader's arm, like a drunk, and say, "And then I did this and it was so interesting." I don't write for that reason.

—ANNIE DILLARD

"Novels are concealed autobiography": Insofar as writing goes, the writer's fundamental attempt is to understand the meaning of his own experiences. If he can't break through to those issues that concern him deeply, he's not going to be very good.

—ROBERT PENN WARREN

(*See Confessions, Self-Revelation.*)

B

BEGINNING

For a true writer each book should be a new beginning where he tries again for something that is beyond attainment. He should always try for something that has never been done or that others have tried and failed. Then sometimes, with great luck, he will succeed. How simple the writing of literature would be if it were only necessary to write in another way what has been well written. It is because we have had such great writers in the past that a writer is driven far out past where he can go, out to where no one can help him.

> —ERNEST HEMINGWAY, in
> recorded address, accepting the
> Nobel Prize for Literature, 1954

Writing is an exploration. You start from nothing and learn as you go.

> —E. L. DOCTOROW

The idea is to get the pencil moving quickly. . . . Once you've got some words looking back at you, you can take two or three— throw them away and look for others.

> —BERNARD MALAMUD

I believe the main thing in beginning a novel is to feel, not that you can write it, but that it exists on the far side of a gulf, which words can't cross: that it's to be pulled through only in a breathless anguish. Now when I sit down to write an article, I have a net of words which will come down on the idea certainly in an hour or so. But a novel . . . to be good should seem, before one writes it, something unwriteable; but only visible; so that for nine months one lives in despair, and only when one has forgotten what one meant does the book seem tolerable.

—Virginia Woolf

One day I seemed to shut a door between me and all publishers' addresses and book lists. I said to myself, Now I can write. Now I can make myself a vase like that which the old Roman kept at his bedside and wore the rim slowly away with kissing it. So I, who had never had a sister and was fated to lose my daughter in infancy, set out to make myself a beautiful and tragic little girl.

—William Faulkner

As the tennis player rallies before the game begins, so must the writer. And as the tennis player is not concerned with where those first balls are going, neither must the writer be concerned with the first paragraph or two. All you're doing is warming up; the rhythm will come. The first moments are critical. You can sit there, tense and worried, freezing the creative energies, or you can start writing *something,* perhaps something silly. It simply doesn't matter *what* you write; it only matters *that* you write. In five or ten minutes the imagination will heat, the tightness will fade, and a certain spirit and rhythm will take over.

—Leonard S. Bernstein

(*See Openings, Story.*)

BELIEFS

Be in love with yr life
Be crazy dumbsaint of the mind
Blow as deep as you want to blow
Write what you want bottomless from the bottom of the mind
Remove literary, grammatical and syntactical inhibition
Write in recollection and amazement for yourself

—JACK KEROUAC

(*See Aim, Purpose, Self-Revelation.*)

BIOGRAPHICAL NOVEL

I know that for the most part if you stay with a thing long enough you can find it, documentation that no one else has ever found. . . . In order to determine whether it will make a biographical novel, I first have to determine whether or not I can understand this person, grasp him, whether I can realize his values, whether I can live through his adventures, experiences, his failures, weaknesses, his faults, his errors, his collapses, as well as his successes, his ecstasies, accomplishments, realizations.

—IRVING STONE

BIOGRAPHY

If the biographer writes from personal knowledge, and makes haste to gratify the publick curiosity, there is danger lest his interest, his fear, his gratitude, or his tenderness, overpower his fidelity, and tempt him to conceal, if not to invent. There are many who think it an act of piety to hide the faults or failings of their friends,

31

even when they can no longer suffer by their detection, but therefore see whole ranks of characters adorned with uniform panegyrick, and not to be known from one another, but by extrinsick and casual circumstances. "Let me remember," says Hale, "when I find myself inclined to pity a criminal, that there is likewise a pity due to the country." If there is a regard due to the memory of the dead, there is yet more respect to be paid to knowledge, to virtue, and to truth.

—SAMUEL JOHNSON

Then you take it all—the chronology, the letters, the interviews, your worn knowledge, the newspaper cuttings, the history books, the diary, the thousand hours of contemplation, and you try to make a whole of it, not a chronicle but a drama, with a beginning and an end, the whole being given form and integrity because a man moves through it from birth to death, through all the beauty and terror of human life.

—ALAN PATON

A writer is always going to betray somebody. If you're going to be honest with your subject, you can't be genteel.

—TED MORGAN

[The biographer] must be as ruthless as a board meeting smelling out embezzlement, as suspicious as a secret agent riding the Simplon-Orient Express, as cold-eyed as a pawnbroker viewing a leaky concertina.

—PAUL MURRAY KENDALL

To preserve . . . a becoming brevity—a brevity which excludes everything that is redundant and nothing that is significant—that surely is the first duty of the biographer. The second, no less surely, is to maintain his own freedom of spirit. It is not his business to be complimentary; it is his business to lay bare the facts of the case, as he understands them . . . dispassionately, impartially, and without ulterior intentions. To quote the words of a Master—*"Je n'impose rien; je ne propose rien; j'expose."*

—LYTTON STRACHEY

In writing biography, fact and fiction shouldn't be mixed. And if they are, the fiction parts should be printed in red ink, the fact parts in black ink.

—CATHERINE DRINKER BOWEN

A biographer's first duty is to recover the actual; and what is more powerful in a man's life than the detail of his days? I take real comfort and instruction in Dr. Johnson's statement to Boswell: "Sir, nothing is too little for so little a creature as man." And I confess to feeling an odd little private thrill when I found a ragged notebook that included Roger Casement's laundry list for the 12th of May in 1899 in Loanda on the west coast of Africa. I felt my nostrils flaring: I had been granted a quick intimation that seemed to be olfactory, a whiff of the real dailiness of a British consul's life in tropical parts and Victorian times.

—B. L. REID

In the new biography, life illuminates art. The biographer's task is to reveal the work's emotional genesis, to anatomize the private and public events that brought it into being. Biography is a form of textual interpretation—the life as a key to the work. George Painter has even argued that we can't properly read Proust's novel until we know the life Proust lived: "The biographer must discover, beneath the mask of the artist's everyday, objective life, the secret life from which he extracted his work."

—JAMES ALLAN

A good biography is prompted not by the inherent qualities of the subject, but by the biographer's consciously or unconsciously realized opportunity for self-expression. The features in a biography are all distinct enough and they are recognizably the features of the subject; but the hunted eyes and the hunting nose, the wafer-thin mouth and rocky chin are the biographer's own.

—JULIAN SYMONS

The trawling net fills, then the biographer hauls it in, sorts, throws back, stores, fillets and sells. Yet consider what he doesn't catch; there is always far more of that. The biography stands, fat and worthyburgherish on the shelf, boastful and sedate; a shilling life will give you all the facts, a 10-pound one all the hypotheses as well. But think of everything that got away, that fled with the last deathbed exhalation of the biographee. We can study files for decades, but every so often we are tempted to throw up our hands and declare that history is merely another literary genre, the past is autobiographical fiction pretending to be a parliamentary report.

—JULIAN BARNES

(See Biographical Novel, Historical Novels, Historical Writing, Hurt Feelings.)

BOREDOM

Beware of creating tedium! I know no guard against this so likely to be effective as the feeling of the writer himself. When once the sense that the thing is becoming long has grown upon him, he may be sure that it will grow upon his readers.

—ANTHONY TROLLOPE

In everything, no matter what it may be, uniformity is undesirable. Leaving something incomplete makes it interesting, and gives one the feeling that there is room for growth.

—YOSHIDA KENKO

The fact that many people should be shocked by what he writes practically imposes it as a duty upon the writer to go on shocking them.

—ALDOUS HUXLEY

I want the reader to turn the page and keep on turning to the end. This is accomplished only when the narrative moves steadily ahead, not when it comes to a weary standstill, overloaded with every item uncovered in the research.

—BARBARA TUCHMAN

(*See inclusiveness, Interest, Pace.*)

BRAINSTORMING

The purpose of brainstorming is to stimulate creative thought. . . . When you come up with an idea or a phrase that isn't quite right, resist the temptation to throw it out and start again. Just write it down. . . . Don't try to write "polished prose." . . . Don't stop to perfect spelling, grammar, or even phrasing. Keep working at the level of ideas . . . try to keep your eye on the question or the problem you have set for yourself. Brainstorming is not free association; it is a goal-directed effort to discover ideas relevant to your problem.

—LINDA FLOWER

(*See Creativity, Ideas, Originality.*)

C

CAREER PATH

Be a scribe! Your body will be sleek, your hand will be soft. . . . You are one who sits grandly in your house; your servants answer speedily; beer is poured copiously; all who see you rejoice in good cheer. Happy is the heart of him who writes; he is young each day.

—PTAHOTEP, 4500 B.C.

Ask yourself in the quietest hour of your night: *must* I write? Dig down into yourself for a deep answer. And if this should be in the affirmative, if you may meet this solemn question with a strong and simple, *I must,* then build your life according to this necessity.

—RAINER MARIA RILKE, *Letters to a Young Poet*

(*See Writing Workshops.*)

CHALLENGE

The function of a writer is to produce a masterpiece and . . . no other task is of any consequence.

—CYRIL CONNOLLY

There is no use writing anything that has been written before unless you can beat it. What a writer in our time has to do is write what hasn't been written before or beat dead men at what they have done.

—ERNEST HEMINGWAY

If there's a book you really want to read but it hasn't been written yet, then you must write it.

—TONI MORRISON

I seemed to see that this life that we live in half-darkness can be illumined, this life that at every moment we distort can be restored to its true pristine shape, that a life, in short, can be realised within the confines of a book! How happy would he be, I thought, the man who had the power to write such a book! What a task awaited him! . . . This writer would have to prepare his book with meticulous care, perpetually regrouping his forces like a general conducting an offensive, and he would have also to endure his book like a form of fatigue, to accept it like a discipline, build it up like a church, follow it like a medical regimen, vanquish it like an obstacle, win it like a friendship, cosset it like a little child, create it like a new world without neglecting those mysteries whose explanation is to be found probably only in worlds other than our own and the presentiment of which is the thing that moves us most deeply in life and in art.

—MARCEL PROUST

(*See Aim, Dedication, Purpose, Values.*)

CHANCE

Chance is the world's greatest novelist. If you would be a prolific writer, just study it closely.

—HONORÉ DE BALZAC

CHARACTERIZATION

When I write, I live with my characters. It's like going to work. You see the people at the next desk in full regalia all the time, and you know where they came from and where they are going. The point is to define the nuances of everything that's happening with them and to find the element of their lives that is fascinating enough to record. That takes a lot of doing.

—WILLIAM KENNEDY

You can never know enough about your characters. Biographies and reminiscences, technical works, will give you often an intimate detail, a telling touch, a revealing hint, that you might never have got from a living model. People are hard to know. It is a slow business to induce them to tell you the particular thing about themselves that can be of use to you. They have the disadvantage that often you cannot look at them and put them aside, as you can a book, and you have to read the whole volume, as it were, only to learn that it had nothing much to tell you.

—W. SOMERSET MAUGHAM

The moment comes when a character does or says something you hadn't thought about. At that moment he's alive and you leave it to him.

—GRAHAM GREENE

I would never write about someone who is not at the end of his rope.

—STANLEY ELKIN

Start with character. *Choose the person you want.* When you've chosen him, ask yourself these questions:

1. What does this person want?
2. What prevents him from getting it?
3. What does he do about this obstacle?
4. What are the results of what he does?
5. What showdown does all this lead to?
6. Does he get what he wants, finally, or does he not?
7. Now—exactly what have I *said?*

I guarantee this recipe.

—ELOISE JARVIS McGRAW

Every human being has hundreds of separate people living under his skin. The talent of a writer is his ability to give them their separate names, identities, personalities and have them relate to other characters living with him.

—MEL BROOKS

If you are inclined to leave your character solitary for any considerable length of time, better question yourself. Fiction is association, not withdrawal.

—A. B. GUTHRIE, JR.

I *want* people to feel good about life. I hate to walk away from a book or a movie feeling that life isn't worth a damn. People don't need that. I think, maybe most of all, they get hope from my books. The characters are in a difficult situation, and they don't get off scot-free, but they prevail. The secret is to create people whom readers can care about. I do an enormous amount of groundwork on them. I know my characters. I know where they came from, who their grandmothers were, how their parents treated them when they were little. It's the characters' history that makes them who they are, and my characters are very real . . . people relate to them and their relationships.

—DANIELLE STEEL

Advice to young writers who want to get ahead without any annoying delays: don't write about Man, write about *a* man.

—E. B. WHITE

When writing a novel a writer should create living people; people, not characters. A *character* is a caricature.

—ERNEST HEMINGWAY

Characters must *materialize*—i.e., must have a palpable physical reality. They must be not only seeable (visualizable); they must be to be felt. Power to give physical reality is probably a matter of the extent and nature of the novelist's physical sensibility, or susceptibility.

—ELIZABETH BOWEN

I visualize the characters completely; I have heard their dialogue. I know how they speak, what they want, who they are, nearly everything about them.

—JOYCE CAROL OATES

The writer must let his fingers run out of the story of his characters, who, being only human and full of strange dreams and obsessions, are only too glad to run.

The time will come when your characters will write your stories for you, when your emotions, free of literary cant and commercial bias, will blast the page and tell the truth.

Remember: *Plot* is no more than footprints left in the snow *after* your characters have run by on their way to incredible destinations. *Plot* is observed after the fact rather than before. It cannot precede action. It is the chart that remains when an action is through.

—RAY BRADBURY

Do not be nice to your characters; slap them with one problem after the other. What is compelling about a nice, smart, handsome, rich man? But an illegitimate woman who has lied her way to a conservative congressional seat—now there's a story. Throw in a few reporters, a disgusted husband, a disturbed child or two, and the conflict will carry this story to its heartbreaking/heartwarming conclusion.

   Writing is not like parenting. Torment, confusion, obstacles, and catastrophes are good things.

—ROMELDA SHAFFER

If you want to get to know your characters better, ask yourself: *"How would they behave in a quarrel?"*

—BARNABY CONRAD

The personages in a tale shall be alive, except in the case of corpses, and . . . always the reader shall be able to tell the corpses from the others.

—MARK TWAIN

(*See Coherence, Flaw of Character, Focus, Protagonist.*)

CHILDREN'S BOOKS

"First do no harm," says the Hippocratic oath for physicians. If writers of children's books had to take an oath it might begin, "First tell the truth." Children are tougher than adults think they are, and considerably wiser. They know when they are being lied to, condescended to, equivocated with; they know a fudged fact when they see one.

—WILLIAM ZINSSER

You must write for children in the same way as you do for adults, only better.

—MAXIM GORKY

Young children like books about animals, monsters and machines. They also like predictable plot lines and books with many illustrations. Picture books are visual literature; they stimulate a child's imagination, introduce children to beginnings, middles and ends and extend the experience of their worlds.

As children grow older, they are more likely to become interested in nonfiction or stories that perceptively mirror themselves.

—STEPHANIE LOER

CLARITY

I see but one rule: to be clear. If I am not clear, all my world crumbles to nothing.

—STENDHAL to Balzac

When a man has something to say he must try to say it as clearly as possible, and when he has nothing to say it is better for him to keep quiet.

—Leo Tolstoy to an anonymous
young poet

To a beginner, the advice I would give would be to think straight and write simply. To be clear is the first duty of a writer; to charm and to please are graces to be acquired later.

—Brander Matthews

The Principles of Clear Statement:

It should always be made clear who is addressing whom, and on the subject of whom.

It should always be made clear which of two or more things already mentioned is being discussed.

Every unfamiliar subject or concept should be clearly defined; and neither discussed as if the reader knew about it already nor stylistically disguised.

There should never be any doubt left as to where something happened or is expected to happen.

There should never be any doubt left as to when.

—Robert Graves and Alan
Hodge

NOTE: *Consider how much more forceful these principles would be if stated in the active voice.*

You credit William Cobbett with the quip: "He who writes badly thinks badly." Cobbett was not the first to say that; it was

Pericles. He wrote: "The man who can think and does not know how to express what he thinks is at the level of him who cannot think." Those who want to learn to write with precision, grace, color and clarity should read *aloud* Plato, Montaigne, Voltaire and Proust.

—PAUL MOSCANYI

What can be said at all, can be said clearly.

—LUDWIG WITTGENSTEIN

An excellent precept for writers: have a clear idea of all the phrases and expressions you need, and you will find them.

—XIMÉNÈS DOUDAN

Take care to avoid getting asked the favorite question of Harold Ross, *The New Yorker*'s late editor: "What the hell do you mean?"

—KATHLEEN KRULL

(*See Accuracy, Details, Precision.*)

CLICHÉS

The writer who aims at producing the platitudes which are "not for an age but for all time" has his reward in being unreadable in all ages.

—GEORGE BERNARD SHAW

One can at least change one's own habits, and from time to time one can even, if one jeers loudly enough, send some worn out and useless phrase—some *jackboot, Achilles' heel, hotbed, melting pot, acid test, veritable inferno* or other lump of verbal refuse—into the dustbin where it belongs.

—George Orwell

If a writer litters his prose with platitudes—if every idea is first and foremost and in the last analysis one that hits the nail on the head—we can safely infer that the writer lacks an instinct for what gives language its freshness. . . . What exactly is wrong with "the top brass"? Nothing—and everything. Taste is knowing that it's better to call people in authority what they are: officials or executives or the president of the company. Non-taste reaches for the cute synonym.

—William Zinsser

Anyone who writes of the American Revolutionary period must beware of buckled shoes, quill pens and night watchmen calling the hour.

—Catherine Drinker Bowen

COHERENCE

A good story should have coherence and sufficient probability for the needs of the theme; it should be of a nature to display the development of character, which is the chief concern of fiction at the present day, and it should have completeness, so that when it is finally unfolded no more questions can be asked about the persons who took part in it. It should have, like Aristotle's tragedy, a beginning, a middle, and an end.

—W. Somerset Maugham

The main difference between living people and fictitious characters is that the writer takes great pains to give the characters coherence and inner unity, whereas the living people may go to extremes of incoherence because their physical existence holds them together.

—HUGO VON HOFMANNSTHAL

(*See Characterization.*)

COMPASSION

When you depict sad or unlucky people, and want to touch the reader's heart, try to be colder—it gives their grief, as it were, a background, against which it stands out in greater relief. As it is, your heroes weep and you sigh. Yes, you must be cold.

—ANTON CHEKHOV

(*See Sympathy.*)

COMPLEXITY

It is not a permanent necessity that poets should be interested in philosophy, or in any other subject. We can only say that it appears likely that poets in our civilization, as it exists at present, must be *difficult*. Our civilization comprehends great variety and complexity, and this variety and complexity, playing upon a refined sensibility, must produce various and complex results.

—T. S. ELIOT

(*See Obscurity, Subtlety.*)

COMPOSITION

So far as the art of composition can be taught, it seems to me to depend upon a knowledge of the elementary rules of grammar and rhetoric, and familiarity with good literature. Beyond that, it depends upon the man himself, the intellectual and aesthetic condition into which he brings himself. . . . I have a friend who does not know a rule of grammar, but writes perfect and elegant English simply by the force of a clear mind, a fine nature, and a good ear. My own rule would be: Be something, know something, feel truly, practice, and then let the style be what it will. It will reflect the man, and that is the true end of composition.

—THEODORE F. MUNGER

COMPROMISES

If you alter your writing to pander to a market trend—or a supposed trend—then you're compromising your craft, number one, and number two, you're no longer a writer, you're a hack. The only concession a writer should make to the market is to maintain a contemporary style and viewpoint, since there's no market for Victorian prose. Be aware of what's going on in the world so you don't make outrageous *faux pas* about things. If you know nothing about rock 'n' roll, find out something about it. Do your research.

—JAMES KISNER

CONCISENESS

In composing, as a general rule, run your pen through every other word you have written; you have no idea what vigor it will give to your style.

—SYDNEY SMITH

In all pointed sentences, some degree of accuracy must be sacrificed to conciseness.

—SAMUEL JOHNSON

Vigorous writing is concise. A sentence should contain no unnecessary words, a paragraph no unnecessary sentences, for the same reason that a drawing should have no unnecessary lines and a machine no unnecessary parts.

—WILLIAM STRUNK, JR.

E. B. White said that Professor Strunk used to grab his coat lapels in class and say, "OMIT NEEDLESS WORDS, OMIT NEEDLESS WORDS, OMIT NEEDLESS WORDS." Everything three times, and I am sure it did no harm to his writing students in 1920. Neither does SHOW, DON'T TELL.

—JUDY DELTON

[On being asked whether he felt constrained]: I do, but that great quote of Stravinsky's always comes to me when I think of that. He said, "Given an infinity of possibilities, I could do nothing."

The business of any artwork—if I can refer to my stuff generally as art—is synthesis. If you have a novel, the idea is to condense it and get something said in less time than it took to live it.

—ANDY ROONEY

The writer who loses his self-doubt, who gives way as he grows old to a sudden euphoria, to prolixity, should stop writing immediately: the time has come for him to lay aside his pen.

—COLETTE

Be clear. Be concise. Be forceful. Know where you're going. Avoid windy locutions, repetitive mannerisms. Save your most important point for last.

—WILLIAM STRUNK, JR.

(*See Cutting, Editing, Sentences.*)

CONCRETE VS. ABSTRACT

Writing too largely in abstract terms is one of the worst and most widespread of literary faults. It sounds learned, it saves the writer from having to use his eyes and ears, and it makes slovenly thinking possible because it does not require definiteness . . . never use an abstract term if a concrete one will serve. Appeal directly to your reader's emotions rather than indirectly through the intermediary of an intellectualizing process. Tell him that the man *gave a dollar to the tramp* rather than that he *indulged in an act of generosity.*

Abstract: *Mortal existence is characterized by its transitoriness and its fallacious appearance of importance.*

Concrete: *All the world's a stage, and all the men and women merely players.*

—DAVID LAMBUTH

The abstract is seldom as effective as the concrete. "She was distressed" is not as good as, even, "She looked away."

—JOHN GARDNER

An abstract style is always bad. Your sentences should be full of stones, metals, chairs, tables, animals, men and women.

—ALAIN (Émile Chartier)

CONDESCENSION

One must not "write down" to his audience. The sense of over-simple statement and painfully careful explanation can disgust the reader as quickly as any offense of which the writer is capable. Prose which is properly suited to an audience of eight-year-olds would prove completely tiresome, or, on the other hand, unintentionally funny, to a mature audience. Swift, for example, would have adopted a very different tone, had *Drapier's Letters* been addressed to a lettered audience.

—CLEANTH BROOKS and ROBERT
PENN WARREN

A condescending, disdainful tone towards little people, only because they are little, does no credit to the human heart. In literature low ranks are as indispensable as in the army—thus speaks the head, and the heart must say it even more emphatically.

—ANTON CHEKHOV

No writer can improve his work until he discards the dulcet notion that the reader is feebleminded, for writing is an act of faith, not a trick of grammar. Ascent is at the heart of the matter . . . a writer who questions the capacity of the person at the other end of the line is not a writer at all, merely a schemer.

—E. B. WHITE

You must be aware that your reader is at least as bright as you are.

—WILLIAM MAXWELL's maxim

CONFESSIONS

[Nathaniel] Hawthorne . . . his four romances are full of anguished confessions. In the preface to his *Mosses,* he said: "So far as I am a man of really individual attributes I veil my face; nor am I, nor have I ever been, one of those supremely hospitable people who serve up their own hearts, delicately fried, with brain sauce, as a tidbit for their beloved public." But he also said at the end of *The Scarlet Letter,* when drawing a moral from Mr. Dimmesdale's tragic life: "Be true! Be true! Show freely to the world, if not your worst, yet some trait whereby the worst may be inferred." Divided between his two impulses, toward secrecy and toward complete self-revelation, he achieved a sort of compromise; he revealed himself, but usually under a veil of allegory and symbol.

—MALCOLM COWLEY

CONFLICT

Make sure your main character wants something, and make sure somebody is keeping him from getting it. In *Cat on a Hot Tin Roof* Big Daddy wants a son from Brick. Brick is obstinate. They struggle. Action!

—LAVONNE MUELLER

Good writing obeys the dictum of Horace: "Remember always never to bring a tame in union with a savage thing."—meaning, among other things, don't distract a mystery reader with a romantic subplot.

—FLORENCE KING

(*See Plot.*)

52

CONSCIENCE

To have something to say is a question of sleepless nights and worry and endless ratiocination of a subject—of endless trying to dig out the essential truth, the essential justice. As a first premise you have to develop a conscience and if on top of that you have talent so much the better. But if you have talent without the conscience, you are just one of many thousand journalists.

—F. Scott Fitzgerald

CONTACT WITH READER

Now the purpose of a book I suppose is to amuse, interest, instruct, but its warmer purpose is just to associate with the reader. You use symbols he can understand so that the two of you can be together.... Let's take the inner chapters of *The Grapes of Wrath*. ... You say the inner chapters were counterpoint and so they were—that they were pace changers and they were that too but the basic purpose was to hit the reader below the belt. With the rhythms and symbols of poetry one can get into a reader—open him up and while he is open introduce—things on an intellectual level which he would not or could not receive unless he were opened up. It is a psychological trick if you wish but all techniques of writing are psychological tricks. Perspective in painting is a trick, word sounds are tricks, even arrangement and form are tricks. And a trick is only good if it is effective. The writer never knows whether his trick is going to work until he has a reader.

—John Steinbeck

Writing is simply the writer and the reader on opposite ends of a pencil; they should be as close together as that.

—Jay R. Gould

Give readers a book with people they care about and they will queue up to shake the author's hand.

—NORMAN COUSINS

What really knocks me out is a book that, when you're all done reading it, you wish the author that wrote it was a terrific friend of yours and you could call him up on the phone whenever you felt like it.

—J. D. SALINGER

(*See Duty to Reader, Interpretation.*)

CONTENT

Be daring, take on anything. Don't labor over little cameo works in which every word is to be perfect. Technique holds a reader from sentence to sentence, but only content will stay in his mind.

—JOYCE CAROL OATES

(*See Subject.*)

COPYWRITING

Headlines:

The headline is the "ticket on the meat." Use it to flag down the readers who are prospects for the kind of product you are advertising.
Every headline should appeal to the reader's *self-interest*.

Always try to inject *news* into your headlines, because the consumer is always on the lookout for new products, or new ways to use an old product, or new improvements in an old product. The two most powerful words you can use in a headline are FREE and NEW.

Body Copy:

Don't beat about the bush—go straight to the point. Avoid analogies of the "just as, so too" variety.
Avoid superlatives, generalizations, and platitudes. Be specific and factual. Be enthusiastic, friendly and memorable. Don't be a bore. Tell the truth, but make the truth fascinating.

—DAVID OGILVY

COURAGE

In your writing, be strong, defiant, forbearing. Have a point to make and write to it. Dare to say what you want most to say, and say it as plainly as you can. Whether or not you write well, write bravely.

—BILL STOUT

He [the writer] must teach himself that the basest of all things is to be afraid; and, teaching himself that, forget it forever, leaving no room in his workshop for anything but the old verities and truths of the heart, the old universal truths lacking which any story is ephemeral and doomed—love and honor and pity and pride and compassion and sacrifice.

—WILLIAM FAULKNER

(*See Dedication.*)

CRAFTSMANSHIP

That writer does the most, who gives his reader the *most* knowledge, and takes from him the *least* time.

—CHARLES CALEB COLTON

Most people won't realize that writing is a craft. You have to take your apprenticeship in it like anything else.

—KATHERINE ANNE PORTER

Writing has laws of perspective, of light and shade, just as painting does, or music. If you are born knowing them, fine. If not, learn them. Then rearrange the rules to suit yourself.

—TRUMAN CAPOTE

Men write about war. A woman should be able to write about taking her daughter to her violin lesson ... It's all in how you handle the material. An engagement with language will take that ride to the violin lesson and transform it, just as Joyce's story of one man wandering around Dublin became *Ulysses*.

—KATE BRAVERMAN

(*See Artistry, Professionalism, Revision.*)

CREATIVITY

In order to compose, all you need to do is to remember a tune that no one else has thought of.

—Attributed to ROBERT SCHUMANN

To live *in* the world of creation—to get into it and stay in it—to frequent it and haunt it—to *think* intensely and fruitfully—to woo combinations and inspirations into being by a depth and continuity of attention and meditation—this is the only thing.

—HENRY JAMES

Breslin's Rule: Don't trust a brilliant idea unless it survives the hangover.

—JIMMY BRESLIN

The Genius of Poetry must work out its own salvation in a man: it cannot be matured by law and precept, but by watchfulness in itself. That which is creative must create itself.

—JOHN KEATS

Hitch your unconscious mind to your writing arm.

—DOROTHEA BRANDE

When you begin a picture, you often make some pretty discoveries. You must be on guard against these. Destroy the thing, do it over several times. In each destroying of a beautiful discovery, the artist does not really suppress it, but rather transforms it, condenses it, makes it more substantial. What comes out in the end is the result of discarded finds. Otherwise, you become your own connoisseur. I sell myself nothing.

—PABLO PICASSO

Creativeness often consists of merely turning up what is already there. Did you know that right and left shoes were thought up only a little more than a century ago?

—BERNICE FITZ-GIBBON

(*See Brainstorming, Ideas, Imagination, Originality.*)

CREDOS

1. Make your own characters seem good.
2. Make clear connections between sentences.
3. Don't say too many things at once.
4. Don't get lured off the line of argument.
5. Use short paragraphs rather than long.
6. Avoid monotony.
7. Be simple.
8. Omit needless words.
9. Write less; rewrite more.
10. Variety is courtesy to the reader.

—F. L. LUCAS

Economize. Think of explaining what you have to say clearly, simply and pleasantly to a small mixed group of intelligent people.

Never use a long word when you can find a short one, or a Latin word when you can find a good Old English one.

Suspect yourself of wordiness whenever you see an *of,* a *which* or a *that.* Inspect all areas surrounding any form of *to be.* Never use *exist.*

Make sure that each word really makes sense. No one who had inspected the meaning of his words could have written: "Every seat in the auditorium was filled to capacity."

The important thing is, I think, to pick up each sentence in turn, asking ourselves if we can possibly make it shorter.

—SHERIDAN BAKER

1. Choose a suitable design and hold to it.
2. Make the paragraph the unit of composition.
3. Use the active voice.
4. Put statements in positive form.
5. Use definite, specific, concrete language.
6. Omit needless words.
7. Avoid a succession of loose sentences.
8. Express co-ordinate ideas in similar form.
9. Keep related words together.
10. In summaries, keep to one tense.
11. Place the emphatic words of a sentence at the end.

—WILLIAM STRUNK, JR.

(*See Language, Rules.*)

CRITICISM

When you get down to work, just do the work the best you can. Don't ever think about the public, or the critics, or any of those things. You are a born writer if there ever was one and have no need to worry about whether this new book will be as good as the "Angel," and that sort of thing. If you simply can get yourself into it, as you can, it *will* be as good. I doubt if you will really think of any of the extrinsic matters when you are at work, but if you did, that might make it less good.

—MAXWELL PERKINS, letter to
Thomas Wolfe

John Updike has said that, on reading an unfavorable review of one of his novels, "My ears close up, my eyes go warm, my chest feels thin as an eggshell, my voice churns silently in my stomach." Ah, yes. All right, so it hurts. But it is not a death sentence. It does not say that you will never write a good novel as long as you live.

As novelists—observers or listeners—we of all people should trust our ability to grow and change.

—PHYLLIS REYNOLDS NAYLOR

Listen carefully to first criticisms made of your work. Note just what it is about your work that the critics don't like and cultivate it. That's the only part of your work that's individual and worth keeping.

—JEAN COCTEAU

The writer's duty is to keep on writing, creating memorable Pvt. Prewitts and Sgt. Crofts, and to hell with Ahab. Perhaps the critics are right: this generation may not produce literature equal to that of any past generation—who cares? The writer will be dead before anyone can judge him—but he *must* go on writing, reflecting disorder, defeat, should that be all he sees at the moment, but ever searching for the elusive love, joy, and hope—qualities which, as in the act of life itself, are best when they have to be struggled for, and are not commonly come by with much ease, either by a critic's formula or by a critic's yearning.

—WILLIAM STYRON

Critics . . . are professionals interested in their own careers. The book they criticize is the material for their own successes or failures and it is of secondary importance to them. I know critics who, thinking up a wisecrack, wait happily for a book to come along to apply it to. This is creativeness—not criticism. I don't think I am ill tempered about adverse criticism. It does seem kind of meaningless. But, do you know, you never get over the ability to have your feelings hurt by deliberately cruel and destructive attacks. Even if you know why the attack was made, it still hurts.

—JOHN STEINBECK

(*See Discouragement, Rejection.*)

CURIOSITY

I believe in not quite knowing. A writer needs to be doubtful, questioning. I write out of curiosity and bewilderment ... I've learned a lot I could not have learned if I were not a writer.

—WILLIAM TREVOR

CUTTING

All books are either dreams or swords,
You can cut or you can drug with words.

—AMY LOWELL

I commenced quietly on my own, to prune it down, to mutilate it, to reduce it to skeletal strength. I'm getting a masochistic pleasure out of it. I wipe out whole pages—without even shedding a tear. Out with the balderdash, out with the slush and drivel, out with the apostrophes, the mythologic mythies, the sly innuendos, the vast and pompous learning (which I haven't got!). Out—out—damned fly-spots. . . . What I must do, before blowing out my brains, is to write a few simple confessions in plain Milleresque language. No flapdoodle about the sun going down over the Adriatic! No entomological inquests, no moonlight and flowers. After all, I know only a few things. I've had a few *major* experiences. I'm no Shakespeare, no Hugo, no Balzac.

—HENRY MILLER

Look for the clutter in your writing and prune it ruthlessly. Be grateful for everything you can throw away. Re-examine each sentence that you put on paper. Is every word doing new work? Can any thought be expressed with more economy? Is anything pompous or pretentious or faddish? Are you hanging on to something useless just because you think it's beautiful?

Simplify. Simplify.

—WILLIAM ZINSSER

The most important lesson in the writing trade is that any manuscript is improved if you cut away the fat.

—ROBERT HEINLEIN

(*See Editing, Revision.*)

D

DECONSTRUCTION

If you try to nail anything down, in the novel, either it kills the novel, or the novel gets up and walks away with the nail. . . . Never trust the artist. Trust the tale.

—D. H. Lawrence

DEDICATION

In utter loneliness a writer tries to explain the inexplicable. . . . The writer must believe that what he is doing is the most important thing in the world. And he must hold to this illusion even when he knows it is not true.

—John Steinbeck

I would rather be a fool than a wise-man. I love all men who *dive*. Any fish can swim near the surface, but it takes a great whale to go downstairs five miles or more; & if he don't attain the bottom, why all the lead in Galena can't fashion the plummet that will. I'm not talking about Mr. Emerson now—but of that whole corps of thought-divers, that have been diving & coming up again with bloodshot eyes since the world began.

—HERMAN MELVILLE

I write to understand as much as to be understood. Literature is an act of conscience. It is up to us to rebuild with memories, with ruins, and with moments of grace.

—ELIE WIESEL

They can't yank a novelist like they can a pitcher. A novelist has to go the full nine, even if it kills him.

—ERNEST HEMINGWAY

Life can't ever really defeat a writer who is in love with writing, for life itself is a writer's lover until death—fascinating, cruel, lavish, warm, cold, treacherous, constant.

—EDNA FERBER

(*See Aim, Courage, Discouragement, Effort, Persistence, Purpose.*)

DETAILS

Caress the detail, the divine detail.

—VLADIMIR NABOKOV

Don't fake it. Irving Stone, who usually does meticulous research on even the smallest details, once thought to inject a little color into his biography of Rachel Jackson. He put flocks of starlings into Tennessee in the early 1800s. He received hundreds of letters from bird-watchers who informed him that starlings hadn't been imported from Europe until the 1890s.

—JAMES J. KILPATRICK

No detail must be neglected in art, for a button half-undone may explain a whole side of a person's character. It is absolutely essential to mention that button. But it has to be described in terms of the person's inner life, and attention must not be diverted from important things to focus on accessories and trivia. Applying this principle, [Tolstoy] notes the physical peculiarities of the people in passing, characterizes old Korchagin by his "bull's neck," Mazlenikov by his "white, fat fist," Katyusha Mazlova by her eyes as dark as wet black currants and her slight squint, Missy by her tapered thumbnail.

—HENRI TROYAT

There is an accuracy that defeats itself by the overemphasis of details. I often say that one must permit oneself, and quite advisedly and deliberately, a certain margin of misstatement.

—BENJAMIN N. CARDOZO

I consider myself an impressionist, because I work by little touches. I believe a ray of sun on a nose is as important as a deep thought.

—GEORGES SIMENON

Short stories can be rather stark and bare unless you put in the right detail. Details make stories human, and the more human a story can be, the better.

—V. S. PRITCHETT

Don't generalize. Use specific images. Avoid abstractions. Be concrete. There is one thing that makes [Sinclair Lewis's] books classics, makes them absolutely memorable. It is his imagery—his very specific images. It makes his writing readable because you can *feel* the restaurant [Billy's Lunch Counter] with the sticky oilcloth on its tables. . . . "Thick handleless cups on the wet oilcloth-covered counter. An odor of onions and the smoke of hot lard. In the doorway a young man audibly sucking a toothpick. An aluminum ashtray labeled, 'Greetings from Gopher Prairie.' "

—JUDY DELTON

(*See Accuracy, Imagery.*)

DIALOGUE

All dialogue should come out of character. It should never come from the author. If a character speaks in slang, then it is perfectly proper to let him do so. It would obviously be out of place to put slang in the mouth of a character to whom such language would be alien. If you want dialogue to be strong and vivid, make it *real*. . . . If you really know your characters, you will know exactly how they should speak.

—SIDNEY SHELDON

How do you write vital, meaningful dialogue that deepens characterization, furthers the plot, expands the theme, and sounds real? Let your characters do the talking. "Frankly, my dear, I don't give a damn!" So spoke Rhett to Scarlett in one of the best-known lines of dialogue ever written. With that statement he signified the end of his patience, his tolerance and maybe even his love.

—EVE BUNTING

NOTE: *In the book* Gone With the Wind, *Margaret Mitchell wrote: "My dear, I don't give a damn." Clark Gable added "Frankly," in the 1939 movie (screenplay by Sidney Howard).*

—*Time* Magazine

The vital dialogue is that exchanged by characters whom their creator has really vitalized, and only the significant passages of their talk should be recorded, in high relief against the narrative.

—EDITH WHARTON

1. Dialogue should be brief.
2. It should add to the reader's present knowledge.
3. It should eliminate the routine exchanges of ordinary conversation.
4. It should convey a sense of spontaneity but eliminate the repetitiveness of real talk.
5. It should keep the story moving forward.
6. It should be revelatory to the speaker's character, both directly and indirectly.
7. It should show the relationships among people.

—ELIZABETH BOWEN

Dialogue in fiction should be reserved for the culminating moments and regarded as the spray into which the great wave of narrative breaks in curving toward the watcher on the shore.

—EDITH WHARTON

Tender [*Is the Night*] is less interesting toward the climax because of the absence of conversation. The eye flies for it and skips essential stuff for they don't want their characters resolved in dessication [*sic*] and analysis but like me in action that results from the previous. All the more reason for *emotional planning*.

—F. Scott Fitzgerald

(*See Language, Playwriting, Screenwriting, Slang, Words.*)

DIRECTION

Whatever you write should, on the surface, out of respect for the sources from which you borrow, and for the sake of language, offer a sense of direction.

—Stéphane Mallarmé

DISCIPLINE

Six hours of uninterrupted writing produces several thousand words. And when a book takes something like five months solid merely to write, well, you have to be disciplined and adhere to a strict routine. You have to keep fit, you need a good diet and the right kind of exercise.

—Paul Johnson

The discipline of the writer is to learn to be still and listen to what his subject has to tell him.

—Rachel Carson

Writing—especially novels—is as much discipline as it is desire. Set time aside each day, or select days each week, and write. Don't wait until you're inspired, because if you do, you'll never finish anything.

—CHRISTOPHER A. BOHJALIAN

It is wise . . . to have not simply a set time for writing—it need not be daily and yet be regular—but also a set "stint" for the day, based on a true, not vainglorious estimate of your powers. Then, when you come to a natural stop somewhere near the set amount, you can knock off with a clear conscience.

—JACQUES BARZUN

I hold my inventive capacity on the stern condition that it must master my whole life, often have complete possession of me, make its own demands on me, and sometimes for months together put everything else away from me. . . . Whoever is devoted to an Art must be content to deliver himself wholly up to it and to find his recompense in it.

—CHARLES DICKENS

Discipline. Tightness. Firmness. Crispness. Sternness. And sternness in our lives. Life is tons of discipline. Your first discipline is your vocabulary; then your grammar and your punctuation, you see. Then, in your exuberance and bounding energy you say you're going to add to that. Then you add rhyme and meter. And your delight in *that* power.

—ROBERT FROST

The most important thing for a writer is to be locked in a study . . . I usually write in my office on the third floor of the house. I write every day from about nine in the morning to one in the afternoon.

I set myself to the task of writing ten pages a day in longhand, which comes out to about five typewritten pages. The rest of the day I spend talking on the phone with my publishers, promoting my books and answering my mail.

—ERICA JONG

What is needed is, in the end, simply this: solitude, great inner solitude. Going into yourself and meeting no one for hours on end—that is what you must be able to attain. To be alone, as you were alone in childhood, when the grown-ups were going about, involved in things which seemed important and great, because the great ones looked so busy and because you grasped nothing of their business.

—RAINER MARIA RILKE

Artists don't talk about art. Artists talk about work. If I have anything to say to young writers, it's stop thinking of writing as art. Think of it as work. . . . It's hard physical work. You keep saying, "No, that's wrong, I can do it better." You have an original, fresh concept; you want to fulfill it as precisely and as completely as you can, and in the effort to achieve that, the constant self-demand is, in essence, what art is.

—PADDY CHAYEFSKY

An artist must serve Mammon; he must have "self-concentration"—selfishness, perhaps. You, I am sure, will forgive me for sincerely remarking that you might curb your magnanimity, and be more of an artist, and load every rift of your subject with ore. The thought of such discipline must fall like cold chains upon you, who perhaps never sat with your wings furled for six months together.

—JOHN KEATS to Percy Bysshe
Shelley

Discipline is never a restraint [on creativity]. It's an aid. The first commandment of the romantic school is: "Don't worry about grammar, spelling, punctuation, vocabulary, plot or structure—just let it come." That's not writing; that's vomiting, and it leads to uncontrolled, unreadable prose. Remember: Easy writing makes hard reading, but hard writing makes easy reading.

—FLORENCE KING

(*See Doggedness, Drivenness, Effort, Environment, Persistence, Rules.*)

DISCOURAGEMENT

Don't get discouraged because there's a lot of mechanical work to writing. . . . I rewrote the first part of *A Farewell to Arms* at least fifty times. . . . The first draft of anything is shit. When you first start to write you get all the kick and the reader gets none, but after you learn to work it's your object to convey everything to the reader so that he remembers it not as a story he had read but something that happened to himself. That's the true test of writing. When you can do that, the reader gets the kick and you don't get any. You just get hard work and the better you write the harder it is because every story has to be better than the last one. It's the hardest work there is.

—ERNEST HEMINGWAY

When I face the desolate impossibility of writing five hundred pages a sick sense of failure falls on me and I know I can never do it. This happens every time. Then gradually I write one page and then another. One day's work is all I can permit myself to contemplate and I eliminate the possibility of ever finishing.

—JOHN STEINBECK

I remember that phrase of Whitman's, "Make the work," and I think that's terribly important. It's important not to give up and to keep working. You need a very tough skin because when you send poems out into the world, they can be misunderstood, and it can be very difficult to accept such misunderstanding.

—WILLIAM JAY SMITH

I sit down religiously every morning, I sit down for eight hours every day—and the sitting down is all. In the course of that working day of 8 hours I write 3 sentences which I erase before leaving the table in despair. . . . Sometimes it takes all my resolution and power of self-control to refrain from butting my head against the wall.

—JOSEPH CONRAD

Raymond Chandler, in a 1959 letter defending a weak Hemingway book, likened a champion writer to a baseball pitcher. When the champ has stuff, the great mystery writer wrote, "when he can no longer throw the high hard one, he throws his heart instead. He throws something. He doesn't just walk off the mound and weep."

—TOM NOLAN

(*See Courage, Criticism, Dedication, Doggedness, Effort, Persistence, Rejection.*)

DOGGEDNESS

If you wish to be a writer, write.

—EPICTETUS

A man may write at any time, if he will set himself doggedly to it.

—SAMUEL JOHNSON

The great thing is to last and get your work done and see and hear and learn and understand and write when there is something that you know; and not before; and not too damned much after.

—ERNEST HEMINGWAY

You have to get lucky at some point, but you can only get lucky if you are still on the road, and for each of us that road, that journey is of a different length. The thing is to keep doing it and doing it, any way you can.

—LAWRENCE KASDAN

To be successful you must have talent joined with the willingness, the eagerness, to work like a dog. I write seven days a week from ten until four, and I begrudge every minute I have to spend on the phone or away from my typewriter. Also, you've got to be willing to take a chance on something that could be unsuccessful. Thousands of people plan to be writers, but they never get around to it. The only way to find out if you can write is to set aside a certain period every day *and try*. Save enough money to give yourself six months to be a full-time writer. Work every day and the pages will pile up.

—JUDITH KRANTZ

(*See Discipline, Effort, Persistence.*)

DRAFTS

I just say OK, I'm going to make the biggest fool of myself as possible and just go right ahead and don't stop. I just let it get out. Sometimes I just run out of steam and I don't get the first draft wholly done, and I go back and start again. Often my first draft is a very complete draft. It may not be the one I use or anywhere near what finally takes place. But it's in my own handwriting and very few people can read it but me.

—HORTON FOOTE

Put your notes away before you begin a draft. What you remember is probably what should be remembered; what you forget is probably what should be forgotten. No matter; you'll have a chance to go back to your notes after the draft is completed. What is important is to achieve a draft which allows the writing to flow.

—DONALD M. MURRAY

In writing, you can make a silk purse out of a sow's ear, but first you have to create the sow's ear.
  Your first draft is the sow's ear.

—CHARLES PARNELL

(*See Outlining, Planning.*)

DRINKING AND WRITING

Boozing does not necessarily have to go hand in hand with being a writer. . . . I therefore solemnly declare to all young men trying to be writers that they do not actually have to become drunkards first.

—JAMES JONES

DRIVENNESS

Drivenness is trouble for both the novelist and his friends; but no novelist, I think, can succeed without it. Along with the peasant in the novelist, there must be a man with a whip.

—JOHN GARDNER

Writing doesn't require drive. It's like saying a chicken has to have drive to lay an egg.

—JOHN UPDIKE

(See Doggedness.)

DUTY TO READER

I don't think I've ever written anything that is designed purely as a sop to the reader: I don't put in bits of sex to increase sales. But I always bear him in mind, and try to visualize him and watch for any signs of boredom or impatience to flit across the face of this rather shadowy being, the Reader.

—KINGSLEY AMIS

If we work upon marble it will perish; if on brass, time will efface it; if we rear temples, they will crumble into dust; but if we work upon immortal minds, and imbue them with principles, with the just fear of God and love of our fellow men, we will engrave on those tablets something that will brighten all eternity.

—NOAH WEBSTER

The storyteller of our time, as in any other time, must be an entertainer of the spirit in the full sense of the word, not just a preacher of social and political ideals. Nonetheless, it is also true that the serious writer of our time must be deeply concerned about the problems of his generation. [These, he said, included the decline of the power of religion and the weakening of the family.]

—ISAAC BASHEVIS SINGER

A novel can educate to some extent. But first, a novel has to entertain—that's the contract with the reader: you give me ten hours and I'll give you a reason to turn the page. I have a commitment to accessibility. I believe in plot. I want an English professor to understand the symbolism while at the same time I want one of my relatives—who's never read anything but the Sears catalogue—to read my books.

—BARBARA KINGSOLVER

A writer has the duty to be good, not lousy; true, not false; lively, not dull; accurate, not full of error. He should tend to lift people up, not lower them down.

—E. B. WHITE

Crass stupidities shall not be played upon the reader ... by either the author or the people in the tale.

The personages of a tale shall confine themselves to possibilities and let miracles alone; or, if they venture a miracle, the author must so plausibly set it forth as to make it look possible and reasonable.

The author shall make the reader feel a deep interest in the personages of his tale and in their fate; and that he shall make the reader love the good people in the tale and hate the bad ones.

Use the right word and not its second cousin.

—MARK TWAIN

The author is like the host at a party. It is his party, but he must not enjoy himself so much that he neglects his guests. His enjoyment is not so much his own but theirs.

—CHARLES P. CURTIS

(See Contact with Reader, Interpretation.)

E

EARNESTNESS

Let a man speak with earnestness and promptitude, have something first to communicate, and let him eliminate from his speech all that is loose, needless, and ineffective, and there is style, the pure juice of his nature, in what he says.

—EDMUND GOSSE

I am in earnest—I will not equivocate—I will not excuse—I will not retreat a single inch, and I will be heard!

—WILLIAM LLOYD GARRISON

EDITING

Read over your compositions and whenever you meet with a passage that you think is particularly fine, strike it out.

—SAMUEL JOHNSON'S recollection
of the advice of a college tutor

My own experience is that once a story has been written, one has to cross out the beginning and the end. It is there that we authors do most of our lying . . . one must ruthlessly suppress everything that is not concerned with the subject.

—Anton Chekhov

If you require a practical rule of me, I will present you with this: Whenever you feel an impulse to perpetrate a piece of exceptionally fine writing, obey it—wholeheartedly—and delete it before sending your manuscript to press.

—Arthur Quiller-Couch

Sit down and put down everything that comes into your head and then you're a writer. But an author is one who can judge his own stuff's worth, without pity, and destroy most of it.

—Colette

Analysis, reflection, much writing, ceaseless correction—there is all my secret.

—Johann Sebastian Bach

The next time I'm asked to divulge the magic secret of selling a novel, I intend to say, the secret lies in trusting your reader's imagination. Get rid of the unnecessary clutter. Highlight, condense—everything: backdrops, dialogue, action. Concentrate on playing on your reader's emotions, and his imagination will fill in all you leave out.

—Joan Dial

(*See Cutting, Drafts, Marginal Notes, Revision.*)

EDITORS/PUBLISHERS

On the whole, I have found editors friendly and pleasant, but unpredictable and uncertain and occasionally embarrassing in their desperation. So seldom do they get what they think they want that they tend to become incoherent in their insistent repetition of their needs. A writer does well to listen to them, but not too often, and not for too long.

—JEROME WEIDMAN

It's a damn good story. If you have any comments, write them on the back of a check.

—ERLE STANLEY GARDNER (note
on a manuscript sent to an
editor)

The advance for a book should be at least as much as the cost of the lunch at which it was discussed.

—CALVIN TRILLIN

I believe the writer . . . should always be the final judge. I have always held to that position and have sometimes seen books hurt thereby, but at least as often helped. The book belongs to the author.

—MAXWELL PERKINS

An editor should tell the author his writing is better than it is. Not a lot better, a little better.

—T. S. ELIOT

Just get it down on paper, and then we'll see what to do about it.

—Maxwell Perkins

EFFECT

A skillful literary artist has constructed a tale. If wise, he has not fashioned his thoughts to accommodate his incidents: but having conceived, with deliberate care, a certain unique or single *effect* to be brought out, he then invents such incidents—he then combines such events as may best aid him in establishing this preconceived effect. *If his very initial sentence tends not to the outbringing of this effect, then he has failed in his first step.*

—Edgar Allan Poe

Remember: what lasts in the reader's mind is not the phrase but the effect the phrase created: laughter, tears, pain, joy. If the phrase is not affecting the reader, what is it *doing* there? Make it do its job or cut it without mercy or remorse.

—Isaac Asimov

(*See Focus, Shape of Ideas.*)

EFFORT

Get black on white.

—Guy de Maupassant

The most important thing for a young writer to learn is that writing doesn't come easy: It's work. There's no point in fooling with it unless you have to—unless you have a need to do it.

A publisher friend of mine says that most writers are not real writers, they are just people who "want to have written." Real writers are those who want to write, need to write, have to write.

—ROBERT PENN WARREN

Beginners who are first starting out sometimes try to write a novel but they won't do enough work on it. You only learn to be a better writer by actually writing. I don't know much about creative writing programs. But they're not telling the truth if they don't teach, one, that writing is hard work and, two, that you have to give up a great deal of life, your *personal* life, to be a writer.

—DORIS LESSING

One of the few things I know about writing is this: Spend it all, shoot it, play it, lose it, all, right away, every time. Do not hoard what seems good for a later place in the book, or for another book, give it, give it all, give it now. . . . Some more will arise for later, something better. These things fill from behind, from beneath, like well water. Similarly, the impulse to keep to yourself what you have learned is not only shameful, it is destructive. Anything you do not give freely and abundantly becomes lost to you. You open your safe and find ashes.

—ANNIE DILLARD

Who casts to write a living line, must sweat.

—BEN JONSON, "To the Memory
of My Beloved, The Author
William Shakespeare"

(*See Courage, Discipline, Doggedness, Drivenness, Persistence, Productivity.*)

EMOTION

No tears in the writer, no tears in the reader.

—ROBERT FROST

The artist must work with indifferency—too great interest vitiates his work.

—HENRY DAVID THOREAU

In any really good subject, one has only to probe deep enough to come to tears.

—EDITH WHARTON

How can you write if you can't cry?

—RING LARDNER

When you're a writer, you no longer see things with the freshness of the normal person. There are always two figures that work inside you, and if you are at all intelligent you realize that you have lost something. But I think there has always been this dichotomy in a real writer. He wants to be terribly human, and he responds emotionally, but at the same time there's this cold observer who cannot cry.

—BRYAN MOORE

New writers are often told, "Write what you know." I would broaden that by saying, "Write what you know emotionally."

—MARJORIE FRANCO

You get your readers emotionally involved in your characters by being emotionally involved yourself. Your characters must come alive for you. When you are writing about them, you have to feel all the emotions they are going through—hunger, pain, joy, despair. If you suffer along with them and care what happens to them, so will the reader.

—SIDNEY SHELDON

I think that to write really well and convincingly, one must be somewhat poisoned by emotion. Dislike, displeasure, resentment, fault-finding, imagination, passionate remonstrance, a sense of injustice—they all make fine fuel.

—EDNA FERBER

A writer's eyes, to be clear, must be dry.

—GEORGE DARIEN

The only way of expressing emotion in the form of art is by finding an objective correlative, in other words a set of objects, a chain of events, which shall be the formula of that particular emotion. Such that when the external facts, which must terminate in a sensory experience, are given, the emotion is immediately evoked.

—T. S. ELIOT

Despite the culture, an artist must live without fear of emotion, of other types of consciousness, of suprarational experiences. Whether Americans will loosen up, will embrace life, is anybody's guess. If they don't, you'll spend your life in deep rebellion against your own culture. Let others live in black and white; you must live in Technicolor. And without a subjunctive tense you must still make your reader see the blood at the heart of the ruby.

—RITA MAE BROWN

(See Conflict, Excitement, Plot, Suspense.)

EMPHASIS

A piece of writing may be unified and coherent and still not be effective if it does not observe the principle of EMPHASIS. When this principle is properly observed the intended scale of importance of elements to the discourse is clear to the reader. All cats are black in the dark, but all things should not look alike in the light of a reasonable writer's interest in his subject. To change our metaphor, there is a foreground and a background of interest, and the writer should be careful to place each item in its proper location. Like unity and coherence, emphasis is a principle of organization.

—CLEANTH BROOKS and ROBERT
PENN WARREN

When you say something, make sure you have said it. The chances of your having said it are only fair.

—E. B. WHITE

ENDINGS

Much advice is given about the start of a story, the need to capture the reader's interest with the first line or two. The ending is no less important. . . . There must be an *ending,* something that acts as a fixative.

More than forty years ago I read *The Forsyte Saga.* I still remember the closing line—"He might wish and wish and never get it—the beauty and loving in the world"—and how sorry it made me feel for Soames. Everything the reader has learned about Soames is contained in that single line.

—MARY WALLACE

Life goes on, and for the sake of verisimilitude and realism, you cannot positively give the impression of an ending: you must let something hang. A cheap interpretation of that would be to say that you must always leave a chance for a sequel. People die, love dies, but life does not die, and so long as people live, stories must have life at the end.

—JOHN O'HARA

Any true work of art has got to give you the feeling of reconciliation—what the Greeks would call catharsis, the purification of your mind and imagination—through an ending that is endurable because it is right and true. Oh, not in any pawky individual idea of morality or some parochial idea of right and wrong. Sometimes the end is very tragic because it needs to be. One of the most perfect and marvelous endings in literature—it raises my hair now—is the little boy at the end of *Wuthering Heights,* crying that he's afraid to go across the moor because there's a man and woman walking there.

—KATHERINE ANNE PORTER

I don't think the writer has to know the end before starting a story. If he knows his people, as Poe and Hemingway knew theirs, he can start with some notion of the end, or none at all, and turn his people loose to find it on their own.

—ROBERT TWOHY

Don't be afraid to end your piece of writing when you've said whatever it is you meant to say. This isn't a Fourth of July picnic; you don't need the literary equivalent of a fireworks display so that everyone will know the festivities are over. Let your piece of writing end naturally, and it will look just fine.

> —HERBERT E. MEYER and JILL M.
> MEYER

I always know the ending; that's where I start.

> —TONI MORRISON

Whatever it is you do, the last impression is what people remember. Begin well, with attack and accuracy. Drive it through. But, whatever else, make the end the best. Know exactly what you are aiming for and finish with a bang.

> —ALMA GLUCK, mother of Marcia
> Davenport, to her young
> daughter

I have read every imaginable kind of book all my life, and even before I began to write books I saw an awful lot of books that were very interesting in the beginning. The writer would build up your interest and the scope and drive of the plot, and keep you going halfway or two-thirds or three-quarters of the way through, and all of a sudden—blah. The end was nothing. I was aware of this, if only subconsciously. And when I began to write, the one thing that I knew was: Every single thing you do, all the way through, has got to lead to a sound, inarguable conclusion. And so I developed that habit; I wrote the last line first, and I do so to this day.

> —MARCIA DAVENPORT, at age 87

ENVIRONMENT

If you are a writer you locate yourself behind a wall of silence and, no matter what you are doing, driving a car or walking or doing housework . . . you can still be writing, because you have that space.

—JOYCE CAROL OATES

The ideal view for daily writing, hour on hour, is the blank wall of a cold-storage warehouse. Failing this, a stretch of sky will do, cloudless if possible.

—EDNA FERBER

The actual process of writing . . . demands complete, noiseless privacy, without even music; a baby howling two blocks away will drive me nuts.

—WILLIAM STYRON

A woman must have money and a room of her own if she is to write fiction.

—VIRGINIA WOOLF

(*See Discipline, Method, Solitude, Work Station.*)

ESSAY

Give the mood, and the essay, from the first sentence to the last, grows round it as a cocoon grows round the silkworm.

—ALEXANDER SMITH

(*See Mood, Tone.*)

EXCITEMENT

[Advice to Rudyard Kipling (who was living in Vermont)]:

Don't tell us petty stories of our own pettiness. We have enough little Harvard men to do that. Tell us of things new and strange and novel as you used to do. Tell us of love and war and action that thrills us because we know it not, of boundless freedom that delights us because we have it not. . . . Go back where there are temples and jungles and all manner of unknown things, where there are mountains whose summits have never been scaled, rivers whose sources have never been reached, deserts whose sands have never been crossed.

—WILLA CATHER

Find what gave you emotion; what the action was that gave you the excitement. Then write it down making it clear so that the reader can see it too. Prose is architecture, not interior decoration, and the Baroque is over.

—ERNEST HEMINGWAY

(*See Conflict, Emotion, Plot.*)

EXPERIENCE

Throw yourself into the hurly-burly of life. It doesn't matter how many mistakes you make, what unhappiness you have to undergo. It is all your material. . . . Don't wait for experience to come to you; go out after experience. Experience is your material.

—W. SOMERSET MAUGHAM

I suggest . . . that we do *not* write about what we know. One of the dumbest things you were ever taught was to write about what you know. Because what you know is usually dull. Remember when you first wanted to be a writer? Eight or 10 years old, reading about thin-lipped heroes flying over mysterious viny jungles toward untold wonders? That's what you wanted to write about, about what you *didn't* know. So. What mysterious time and place *don't we know?*

—KEN KESEY

Let your fiction grow out of the land beneath your feet.

—WILLA CATHER

To become a true doctor, the candidate must have passed through all the illnesses that he wants to cure and all the accidents and circumstances that he is to diagnose. Truly I should trust such a man.

—MONTAIGNE

Bring the wisdom of a lifetime to your task. Writing from experience does not, of course, mean transcribing experience. You have the responsibility to sift and shape your material until it makes sense as a unit and until that unit can be fitted into the context of the reader's life.

—JUDITH APPELBAUM

[On preserving a "key experience"]:

I've talked about it abstractly. I'm not going to talk about it in detail because, I'm selfish about it. . . . I want to save it. Someday I really would like to write about it. . . . Hemingway is always

89

saying, "Don't talk about them" [key experiences]. I think what he meant or at least what he means for me is that if you keep an experience and you don't talk about it and it's a crystal experience, it's still very close to you, the moment's still enormously clear to you. You can beam a light through it from many an angle, get many a story, many a chapter of a novel. And, you know, writers are like squirrels. We collect these things that we need to get through the long writing winter, or decade or three decades. But if you talk about it, you explain it, you've used up that particular possibility in yourself to go in many directions from that.

—NORMAN MAILER

(*See Impressions.*)

F

FAME

After all, let us not be too scornful of fame; nothing is lovelier, unless it be virtue.

Achilles exists only thanks to Homer. Take away the art of writing from this world, and most likely you will take away its glory.

—Chateaubriand

Enduring fame is promised only to those writers who can offer to successive generations a substance constantly renewed; for every generation arrives upon the scene with its own particular hunger.

—André Gide

(*See Recognition, Rewards.*)

FICTIONAL REALISM VS. NEO-FABULISM

It seems to me that isms, including Magical Realism and Minimalism, are all honorable alternatives to being realistic.

—JOHN UPDIKE

I see a feast of literature as truly a smorgasbord. I wouldn't want a world in which there were only Balzac and Zola and not Lewis Carroll and Franz Kafka. The idea that because we live in a large and varied country we therefore ought to write the sweeping, panoramic novel is like arguing that our poets all ought to be like Walt Whitman rather than Emily Dickinson.

—JOHN BARTH

[On a writer's responsibility to tackle the larger issues of the day]:

It seems to me imperative that literature enter such arguments because what is being disputed is nothing less than what is the case, what is truth and what untruth, and the battleground is our imagination. If writers leave the business of making pictures of the world to politicians, it will be one of history's great and most abject abdications.

There is a genuine need for political fiction, for books that draw new and better maps of reality, and make new languages with which we can understand the world. [It is necessary, even exhilarating] to grapple with the special problems created by the incorporation of political material, because politics is by turns farce and tragedy.

—SALMAN RUSHDIE

The imaginative artist willy-nilly influences his time. If he understands his responsibility and acts on it—taking the art seriously always, himself never quite—he can make a contribution equal to, if different from, that of the scientist, the politician, and the jurist. The anarchic artist so much in vogue now—asserting with vehemence and violence that he writes only for himself, grubbing the worst seams of life—can do damage. But he can also be so useful in breaking up obsolete molds, exposing shams, and crying out the truth, that the broadest freedom of art seems to me necessary to a country worth living in.

—HERMAN WOUK

(*See Realism.*)

FIGURATIVE EXPRESSION

Figurative expression is the application of words to ideas or things outside the normal range of their meanings. E. B. White speaks of "the broncolike ability of the English language to throw whoever leaps cocksurely into the saddle" ... Thurber says that the psychosemanticist will treat "the havoc wrought by verbal artillery upon the fortress of reason" ... Orwell talks about stereotyped phrases "tacked together like the sections of a prefabricated hen house." ... The invention of apt figures of speech requires a certain quality of mind that not everyone possesses—not even all good prose writers. It is probably better to stick to plain statement than to risk spoiling our prose with poor figures. But figurative language offers rich possibilities.

—WILLIAM R. KEAST and ROBERT
E. STREETER

(*See Metaphor, Simile.*)

FLASHBACKS

Each story will dictate its own rhythms. But a fair principle, albeit one easier to state than to apply, is to continue forward from your opening point until the reader's curiosity about the past outweighs his curiosity about the future.

You won't, in general, insert a flashback right in the middle of fascinating action. That merely frustrates the reader, who is trying to find out what happens next—not what happened a long time ago.

But at a certain moment he will *want* a flashback. He'll want to know how things got like this, what makes these people the way they are. He may require orientation: time, place, relationships. This is the moment—when the story has completed its first advance—to direct the reader's attention to such anterior matters.

—Jonathan Penner

FLAW OF CHARACTER

Front-rank characters should have some defect, some conflicting inner polarity, some real or imagined inadequacy.

—Barnaby Conrad

(*See Characterization.*)

FLOWERY STYLE

I notice that you use plain, simple language, short words and brief sentences. This is the way to write English—it is the modern way, and the best way. Stick to it; don't let fluff and flowers and verbosity creep in. When you catch adjectives, kill most of them—then the rest will be valuable. They weaken when they are close together; they give strength when they are wide apart. An adjective habit, or a wordy, diffuse or flowery habit, once fastened upon a person, is as hard to get rid of as any other vice.

> —MARK TWAIN, writing to a
> schoolboy essayist

(*See Style.*)

FOCUS

The most important thing in a work of art is that it should have a kind of focus, i.e., there should be some place where all the rays meet or from which they issue. And this focus must not be able to be completely explained in words. This indeed is one of the significant facts about a true work of art—that its content in its entirety can be expressed only by itself.

> —LEO TOLSTOY

Keep the story moving. The reader will accept a lot of diversive scenes, if they're diverting enough. But you don't want to do such a good job on this that he forgets the point of the whole thing.

> —LAWRENCE BLOCK

Have common sense and . . . stick to the point.

> —W. SOMERSET MAUGHAM

Experiment with changing your focus. Can you enlarge the focus to make an otherwise esoteric book address a larger group of readers? More often, narrowing the focus of your book may paradoxically increase the number of people who will actually buy it. Narrowing your focus can improve your writing as well, and make your book better overall.

—KATHLEEN KRULL

So much bitterness exists between writers and their publishers, you have to eliminate the distractions. You've got to keep focused.

—JOHN IRVING

(See Effect, Shape of Ideas.)

FOCUS OF CHARACTER

When the writer approaches the rough materials of his story, he must always determine the focus of character, for this is one of the organizing principles of his narrative, one of the things which will give his narrative a form. He asks, *whose story is it?* And before he can answer that question he must answer another question, *whose fate is really at stake?*

—CLEANTH BROOKS and ROBERT
PENN WARREN

(See Characterization.)

FORCEFULNESS

A book ought to be an ice pick to break up the frozen sea within us.

—FRANZ KAFKA

I put *myself,* my experiences, my observations, my heart and soul into my work. I press my soul upon the white paper. The writer who does this may have any style, he or she will find the hearts of their readers. You will see, then, that writing a book involves, not a waste, but a great expenditure of vital force.

—AMELIA E. BARR

It was from Handel that I learned that style consists in force of assertion. If you can say a thing with one stroke, unanswerably you have style; if not, you are at best a *marchande de plaisir,* a decorative litterateur, or a musical confectioner, or a painter of fans with cupids and coquettes. Handel had power.

—GEORGE BERNARD SHAW

FORESHADOWING

If, in the first chapter, you say there is a gun hanging on the wall, you should make quite sure that it is going to be used further on in the story.

—ANTON CHEKHOV

The reader is either directly or indirectly promised that exciting, dramatic, interesting, or important things are going to happen in the novel if he just keeps on reading. . . . In *To Kill a Mockingbird,* there is a *direct* promise to the reader that Bob Ewell will attempt to get back at Atticus Finch. In *Tom Jones,* there is an *indirect* promise that somehow the real mother of Tom will be revealed. In *From Here to Eternity,* the reader is given a *direct* promise that Prewitt is going to try to kill Fatso.

—ROBERT MEREDITH and JOHN FITZGERALD

Don't forget that the audience doesn't want to be surprised any more than you do. It wants to know, in advance, that it's going to be surprised so it can worry itself to that point, imagining.

—KENNETH ATCHITY

(*See Surprise.*)

FORM

Do you still think the novel divides, like Gaul, into three parts— the Idea, the Form, and the Style? If so, you are taking your own first tremulous steps into fiction. You want some maxims for writing? Very well. Form isn't an overcoat flung over the flesh of thought . . . it's the flesh of thought itself. You can no more imagine an Idea without a Form than a Form without an Idea. Everything in art depends on execution: the story of a louse can be as beautiful as the story of Alexander. You must write according to your feelings, be sure those feelings are true, and let everything else go hang. When a line is good, it ceases to belong to any school. A line of prose must be as immutable as a line of poetry.

—JULIAN BARNES, paraphrasing
Flaubert

If you want my real opinion, I think today an exaggerated preponderance is given to form. . . . Basically, I suggest that the method itself establishes the form; that a language is only a logic, a natural and scientific construct. The best writer will not be the one who gallops madly amid hypotheses, but rather the one who marches squarely to the middle of the truth. Actually we are rotten with lyricism; we think quite wrongly that the grand style is composed of startling sublimity, ever close to tumbling over into lunacy. The grand style is composed of logic and clarity.

—EMILE ZOLA

Don't think of literary form. Let it get out as it wants to. Overtell it in the matter of detail—cutting comes later. The form will develop in the telling. Don't make the telling follow a form.

—JOHN STEINBECK

(*See Formulas, Plot, Structure.*)

FORMULAS

I had marked down in my notebook three characteristics a work of fiction must possess in order to be successful:

1. It must have a precise and suspenseful plot.
2. The author must feel a passionate urge to write it.
3. He must have the conviction, or at least the illusion, that he is the only one who can handle this particular theme.

—ISAAC BASHEVIS SINGER

In nearly all good fiction, the basic—all but inescapable—plot form is: A central character wants something, goes after it despite opposition (perhaps including his own doubts), and so arrives at a win, lose, or draw.

—JOHN GARDNER

What does it take to make a best-seller? (According to W. Somerset Maugham): "A little religion . . . a little aristocracy . . . a little sex . . . a little mystery, as summed up by this sentence, 'My God,' cried the Duchess, 'I've been @#$%! But by whom?' "

—LIZ SMITH

Make 'em laugh; make 'em cry; make 'em wait.

—CHARLES READE

I would wish him [the artist] to enlarge his sympathies by patient and loving observation while he grows in mental power. It is in the impartial practice of life, if anywhere, that the promise of perfection for his art can be found, rather than in the absurd formulas trying to prescribe this or that particular method of technique or conception.

—JOSEPH CONRAD

Get a girl in trouble, then get her out again.

—KATHLEEN NORRIS

Cleaning out his desk after he left the Warner Brothers writing factory in Hollywood, co-workers found the fruits of William Faulkner's labor: an empty whiskey bottle and a piece of paper on which he had written, 500 times, "Boy meets girl."

—ROBERT HENDRICKSON

(*See Form, Plot, Structure.*)

FORTITUDE

An absolutely necessary part of a writer's equipment, almost as necessary as talent, is the ability to stand up under punishment, both the punishment the world hands out and the punishment he inflicts upon himself.

—IRWIN SHAW

FREEDOM OF EXPRESSION

Enjoy [the novelist's freedom] as it deserves; take possession of it, explore it to its utmost extent, publish it, rejoice in it. All life belongs to you, and do not listen to those who would shut you up into corners of it and tell you that it is only here and there that art inhabits, or to those who would persuade you that this heavenly messenger wings her way outside of life altogether, breathing a superfine air, and turning away her head from the truth of things. There is no impression of life, no manner of seeing and feeling it, to which the plan of the novelist may not offer a place.

—HENRY JAMES

G

GENRE

The absolute first thing to do when you launch a writing project is to resist the impulse to start writing. You need to relax, to settle down and above all YOU NEED TO THINK. Don't worry about wasting time; it's never a waste of time to get your thoughts in order. Who has asked you to write something? Who will read it? What purpose is the piece of writing intended to serve? To persuade? To inform? To trigger action? Ask yourself all these questions . . . and when you feel you've got it right, then—and only then—should you move on to the first real step in the writing process: the correct category of writing product.

—HERBERT E. MEYER and JILL M.
MEYER

Respect the genre you're writing in. In your effort to put your own stamp on it, don't ignore the established conventions of that genre—or you'll alienate your core audience of loyal buyers.

"The best advice that one can give a writer," says editor Page Cuddy, "is not to condescend to the genre or try to pack a literary idea into a more commercial form in hopes of selling it."

—KATHLEEN KRULL

Don't write stuff you can't handle. If you don't like romantic comedies, don't write *Annie Hall*. You have to always write your best, or you're dead.

—WILLIAM GOLDMAN

Genre is a powerful but dangerous lens. It both clarifies and limits. The writer . . . must be careful not to see life merely in the stereotype with which he or she is most familiar but to look at life with all of the possibilities of the genre in mind.

—DONALD M. MURRAY

I wouldn't hesitate to recommend genre fiction. That's probably the speediest way to get your fiction into print. Within any category there are the important "classy" publications and those that are small or "unimportant." If you write what is mainstream fiction, the markets for short stories aren't as numerous. And I think you almost require some special credentials or an "in" if you're writing a so-called serious novel.

—J. N. WILLIAMSON

GHOSTWRITING

You can't make the Duchess into Rebecca of Sunnybrook Farm. The facts of life are very stubborn things.

—CLEVELAND AMORY, on why he stopped helping the Duchess of Windsor with the writing of her memoirs

GOOD VS. EVIL

In every statement of purpose the author is going to *prove* something about life and the only way he can do this is to *prove that something is good or evil about life* . . . the safest and most productive guide for a novelist lies in his own determination of the nature of good and evil. It may be that he will reflect the traditional past, as, for example, Jane Austen did. Or he may challenge the very bases of his society, as did D. H. Lawrence. In any event, it is of considerable importance that a novelist define good and evil for himself.

—ROBERT C. MEREDITH and JOHN
D. FITZGERALD

I believe that there is one story in the world, and only one, that has frightened and inspired us, so that we live in a Pearl White serial of conflicting thought and wonder. Humans are caught . . . in a net of good and evil. . . . Virtue and vice were warp and woof of our first consciousness and they will be the fabric of our last, and this despite changes we may impose on field and river and mountain, on economy and manners. There is no other story. A man, after he has brushed off the dust and chips of his life, will have left only the hard, clean question: Was it good or evil? Have I done well—or ill?

—JOHN STEINBECK

(*See Human Rights, Moral Position, Theme.*)

GRAMMAR

How may an author best acquire a mode of writing which shall be agreeable and easily intelligible to the reader? He must be correct, because without correctness he can be neither agreeable nor intelligible.

—ANTHONY TROLLOPE

A man's grammar, like Caesar's wife, must not only be pure, but above suspicion of impurity.

—EDGAR ALLAN POE

When strictness of grammar does not weaken expression, it should be attended to. . . . But where, by small grammatical negligences, the energy of an idea is condensed, or a word stands for a sentence, I hold grammatical rigor in contempt.

—THOMAS JEFFERSON, letter to
James Madison

Prefer geniality to grammar.

—H. W. FOWLER

How to write good ("Fumblerules"—mistakes that call attention to the rule):

Avoid run-on sentences that are hard to read.
No sentence fragments.
It behooves us to avoid archaisms.
Also, avoid awkward or affected alliteration.
Don't use no double negatives.
If I've told you once, I've told you a thousand times, "Resist hyperbole."
Avoid commas, that are not necessary.
Verbs has to agree with their subjects.
Avoid trendy locutions that sound flaky.
Writing carefully, dangling participles should not be used.
Kill all exclamation points!!!
Never use a long word when a diminutive one will do.
Proofread carefully to see if you any words out.
Take the bull by the hand, and don't mix metaphors.

Don't verb nouns.
Never, ever use repetitive redundancies.
Last but not least, avoid clichés like the plague.

—WILLIAM SAFIRE

(*See Language.*)

GROWTH

Undertake something that is difficult; it will do you good. Unless you try to do something beyond what you have already mastered, you will never grow.

—RONALD E. OSBORN

GURUS

Really, in the end, the only thing that can make you a writer is the person that you are, the intensity of your feeling, the honesty of your vision, the unsentimental acknowledgement of the endless interest of the life around you and within you. Virtually nobody can help you deliberately—many people will help you unintentionally.

—SANTHA RAMA RAU

(*See Influences.*)

HEALTH

> Dear authors! suit your topics to your strength,
> And ponder well your subject, and its length;
> Nor lift your load, before you're quite aware
> What weight your shoulders will, or will not, bear.
>
> —LORD BYRON

The writer, like a priest, must be exempted from secular labor. His work needs a frolic health; he must be at the top of his condition.

> —RALPH WALDO EMERSON

HISTORICAL NOVELS

My books are based 98 percent on documentary evidence. I spend several years trying to get inside the brain and heart, listening to the interior monologues in their letters, and when I have to bridge the chasms between the factual evidence, I try to make an intuitive leap through the eyes and motivation of the person I'm writing about.

—IRVING STONE

HISTORICAL WRITING

The historian should be fearless and incorruptible; a man of independence, loving frankness and truth; one who, as the poet says, calls a fig a fig and a spade a spade. He should yield to neither hatred nor affection, but should be unsparing and unpitying. He should be neither shy nor deprecating, but an impartial judge, giving each side all it deserves but no more. He should know in his writings no country and no city; he should bow to no authority and acknowledge no king. He should never consider what this or that man will think, but should state the facts as they really occurred.

—LUCIAN (A.D. 120–200)

The writers of universal history will only prove themselves of real value when they are able to answer the essential question of history, "What is power?"

—LEO TOLSTOY

We are not to measure the feelings of one age by those of another. Had Walton lived in our day, he would have been the first to cry out against the cruelty of angling.

—WILLIAM HAZLITT

Historians ought to be precise, truthful, and quite unprejudiced, and neither interest nor fear, hatred nor affection, should cause them to swerve from the path of truth, whose mother is history, the rival of time, the depository of great actions, the witness of what is past, the example and instruction to the present, and monitor to the future.

—CERVANTES

It is right for a good man to love his friends and his country, and to hate the enemies of both. But when a man takes upon him to write history, he must throw aside all such feelings, and be prepared, on many occasions, to extol even an enemy, when his conduct deserves applause; nor should he hesitate to censure his dearest and most esteemed friends, whenever their deeds call for condemnation. For as an animal, if it be deprived of sight, is wholly useless; so if we eliminate truth from history, what remains will be nothing but an idle tale. Now, if we pay a proper regard to truth, we shall not hesitate to stigmatise our friends on some occasions, and to praise our enemies; but it may even be necessary to commend and condemn the same persons, as different circumstances may require. Since it is not to be supposed that those who are engaged in great transactions shall always be pursuing false or mistaken views; nor yet is it probable that their conduct can at all times be free from error. A historian therefore, in all that he relates, should take care to be guided in his judgment by the genuine and real circumstances of every action, without reference to those who may have been engaged in it.

—POLYBIUS (205?–123? B.C.)

Reflect on things past, as wars, negotiations, factions, and the like; we enter so little into those interests, that we wonder how men could possibly be so busy, and concerned for things so transitory: Look on the present times, we find the same humour, yet wonder not at all.

—JONATHAN SWIFT

On interviewing historic personages:

What interested me most was not news, but appraisal. What I sought was to grasp the flavor of a man, his texture, his impact, what he stood for, what he believed in, what made him what he was and what color he gave the fabric of his time.

—JOHN GUNTHER

What makes a good writer of history is a guy who is suspicious. Suspicion marks the real difference between the man who wants to write honest history and the one who'd just rather write a good story.

—JIM BISHOP

These are the building blocks of history and biography. The first commandment of scholar and journalist alike is: Go to the original sources. Get the materials—most of them unpublished—that reveal character, motivation, style and content. The second commandment is: Show, don't tell. . . . If I tell a high school student that Hitler was a raging megalomaniac who wreaked havoc in the world for more than a decade, the student may or may not accept what I say. But if I ask him to read *Mein Kampf* and the findings of the Nuremberg Tribunal—if, in short, I show him who Hitler was—I am much more likely to be believed.

—J. ANTHONY LUKAS

(*See Biography, Hurt Feelings.*)

HONESTY

The writer should respect truth and himself, therefore honesty. . . . In literature, as in life, one of the fundamentals is to find, and be, one's true self. . . . In writing, in the long run, pretense does not work. As the police put it, anything you say may be used in evidence against you. If handwriting reveals character, writing reveals it still more.

Most style is not honest enough. . . . A writer may take to long words, as young men to beards—to impress. But long words, like beards, are often the badge of charlatans. Or a writer may cultivate the obscure, to seem profound. But even carefully muddied puddles are soon fathomed. Or he may cultivate eccentricity, to seem original. But really original people do not have to think about being original—they can no more help it than they can help breathing. They do not need to dye their hair green.

—F. L. Lucas

(See Hurt Feelings, Integrity, Truth.)

HORROR STORY WRITING

I try to terrorize the reader. But if . . . I cannot terrify . . . I will try to horrify, and if I find I cannot horrify, I'll go for the gross-out.

—Stephen King

People want to know why I do this, why I write such gross stuff. I like to tell them I have the heart of a small boy—and I keep it in a jar on my desk.

—Stephen King

You have to make sure that no matter how wacky it is, your terrible threat is believable. . . . Unless it's believable, it won't be frightening, and if it isn't frightening, then you haven't delivered what your reader is looking for. And what your reader is looking for above everything else is fear. Fear is the prime ingredient of all successful horror novels, although naturally you have to fulfill the terrible threat with which you have presented your characters. You can't write about vampires who never get around to sinking their fangs into anybody, or werewolves who don't tear anybody's lungs out.

—Graham Masterton

I used to think horror was what we see in the movies and that horror was a very limited formula type of fiction. Whereas it is not at all. The number of themes, the types of horror you can write, is infinite. Much modern science fiction seems to me to be a regurgitation of old science fiction—though that's not true of all of it, of course. I don't see the type of stretching in science fiction today that you see in the early work of Ellison or Bradbury where they were breaking ground. Actually they were breaking ground for the flexibility of horror.

—James Kisner

HUMAN RIGHTS

We must realize that we cannot escape the common lot of pain, and that our only justification, if one there be, is to speak insofar as we can on behalf of those who cannot.

—Albert Camus

A Russian poet who spent seventeen months in the prison lines in Leningrad under Stalin describes one of her images:

Once someone somehow recognized me. Then a woman standing behind me, her lips blue with cold . . . woke from the stupor that enveloped us, and asked me, whispering in my ear (for we spoke only in whispers): "Could you describe this?" I said, "I can." Then something like a smile glided over what was once her face.

—Anna Akhmatova

(*See Good vs. Evil, Moral Position.*)

HUMOR

My method is to take the utmost trouble to find the right thing to say, and then to say it with the utmost levity.

—GEORGE BERNARD SHAW

When you endeavor to be funny in every line you place an intolerable burden not only on yourself but on the reader. You have to allow the reader to breathe. Whenever George S. Kaufman saw three straight funny lines in a play he was directing, he cut the first two. The fact is that all of us have only one personality, and we wring it out like a dish towel. I don't think you can constantly create a new identity if you're a comic writer. You are who you are.

—S. J. PERELMAN

Let your diverting stories be expressed in diverting terms, to kindle mirth in the melancholick, and heighten it in the gay. Let mirth and humour be your superficial design, tho' laid on a solid foundation, to challenge attention from the ignorant, and admiration from the judicious; to secure your work from the contempt of the graver sort, and deserve the praises of men of sense; keeping your eye still fix'd on the principal end of your project, the fall and destruction of that monstrous heap of ill-contriv'd romances, which, tho' abhorred by many, have so strangely infatuated the greater part of mankind. Mind this and your business is done.

—CERVANTES, the author's preface
to *Don Quixote*

HURT FEELINGS

You have to assume that the act of writing is the most important of all. If you start worrying about people's feelings, then you get nowhere at all.

—NORMAN MAILER

I've very carefully avoided portraying anybody who could be recognized. My fiction, some people think, tends a bit towards caricature or stereotypical characters. It's partly to avoid offending
anybody who might recognize himself. This is a constant problem
to me. I suppose it is to most novelists. There is so much wonderful
material [that] you can't write about without hurting somebody a
lot. It would be much easier to write if you didn't bother about
people's feelings.

—DAVID LODGE

It is immoral not to tell.

—ALBERT CAMUS

(*See Biographical Novel, Biography, Criticism, Historical
Writing, Integrity, Offensiveness, Truth.*)

I

IDEAS

I carry my ideas about me for a long time, often a very long time, before I commit them to writing. My memory is so good that I never forget a theme that has once come to me, even if it is a matter of years. I alter much, reject, try again until I am satisfied. Then, in my head, the thing develops in all directions, and, since I know precisely what I want, the original idea never eludes me. It rises before me, grows, I hear it, see it in all its size and extension, *standing before me* like a cast, and it only remains for me to write it down, which is soon done when I can find the time, for sometimes I take up other work, though I never confuse that with the other. You will ask where I find my ideas: I hardly know. They come uninvited, directly or indirectly. I can almost grasp them with my hands in the open air, in the woods, while walking, in the stillness of the night, early in the morning, called up by moods which the poet translates into words, I into musical tones. They ring and roar and swirl about me until I write them down in notes.

—LUDWIG VAN BEETHOVEN

DORN: Hey—a bit excitable, aren't you? Tears in your eyes—. Now, my point is this. You took your plot from the realm of abstract ideas, and quite right too, because a work of art simply must express some great idea. Nothing can be beautiful unless it's also serious. I say, you are pale.

115

TREPLEV: So you don't think I should give up?
DORN: No. But you must describe only the significant and the eternal.

—ANTON CHEKHOV, *The Seagull*,
Act I

NINA: What are you writing?
TRIGORIN: Nothing, just a note. An idea for a plot. A plot for a short story. A young girl like you has lived all her life by a lake. Like a seagull, she loves the lake, and she's happy and free like a seagull. But a man happens to come along and wrecks her life for want of anything better to do. As happened to this seagull. [The seagull was shot by Treplev.]

—ANTON CHEKHOV, *The Seagull*,
Act II

I often get my ideas not from characters, but from the ideas of what my characters will be involved in. Many people who teach writing teach it by saying you've got to get the character first and then blah, blah, blah . . . that is quite true. Ideas come from other places.

—IRVING WALLACE

Writing is not hard. Just get paper and pencil, sit down, and write it as it occurs to you. The writing is easy—it's the occurring that's hard.

—STEPHEN LEACOCK

When I have an idea, I feel the need to deny it: it is one way of testing it. . . . I am persuaded that if the tree of knowledge were shaken in this way, the good fruit would be saved, the bad fruit discarded.

—ALAIN (EMILE CHARTIER)

Ideas have to be wedded to action; if there is no sex, no vitality in them, there is no action. Ideas cannot exist alone in the vacuum of the mind. Ideas are related to living.

—HENRY MILLER

Be alert every minute for new ideas: . . . Even a minor item in a newspaper or magazine can evoke a big idea. . . . I was reading *The New York Times Sunday Magazine* and scanning a general feature on beauty, not a subject of great interest to me. My eye caught the word "Scarsdale," a neighboring village. I read the few lines that aroused me. . . . The author reported that many fashionable Scarsdale residents were reducing remarkably with a one-page diet sheet obtained from a local doctor. I followed through by sending for a copy. . . . I wrote to the doctor (Herman Tarnower) that I saw an idea for a book in his sheet and had some specific suggestions. He invited me to meet with him. We clicked and co-authored *The Complete Scarsdale Medical Diet,* which has sold over ten million copies worldwide, becoming the bestselling diet book ever.

—SAMM SINCLAIR BAKER

The task of a writer consists in being able to *make* something out of an idea.

—THOMAS MANN

(*See Brainstorming, Creativity, Originality.*)

IDENTITY

Leaders who bob and weave like aging boxers don't inspire confidence—or deserve it. The same thing is true of writers. Sell yourself, and your subject will exert its own appeal. Believe in your own identity and your own opinions. Proceed with confidence, generating it, if necessary, by pure willpower. Writing is an act of ego and you might as well admit it. Use its energy to keep yourself going.

—WILLIAM ZINSSER

(*See Self-Revelation.*)

IMAGERY

An effective and economical way of giving an instant picture of a character is to liken him or her to a famous person, someone whose image everyone is familiar with, be it contemporary, historical, or fictional.

My favorite presidential comparison is humorist James Thurber's remark about his boss at *The New Yorker,* Harold Ross:

He looked like a dishonest Abe Lincoln.

Try to get *that* image out of your mind!

—BARNABY CONRAD

The intensity I am urging not only will enrich our vocabularies and induce more accurate writing, it will also do something else. It will give us images. We look intently at a caterpillar, and perhaps we see a covered wagon. We look closely at a hill of close-cropped stubble, and perhaps we see the head of a fresh-caught recruit in the U.S. Marines. . . . Graham Greene looked intently at a row of crows and he saw old black broken umbrellas.

—James J. Kilpatrick

(*See Details, Imagination.*)

IMAGINATION

Since imagination *cannot create material,* set about systematically to stock your mental storehouse. Cultivate the habit of curiosity as to motives which lead people to do what they do. Observe accurately. Increase the variety of your reading, your contacts with others, your emotional experiences, so that they may furnish richer material for the imagination to work with.

—Hinda Teague Hill

It is a feature of the artistic imagination that it should be able to reconstitute everything on the basis of very limited data. When Delacroix wanted to paint a tiger, he used his cat as a model.

—Henry de Montherlant

Let him mature the strength of his imagination amongst the things of this earth, which it is his business to cherish and know, and refrain from calling down his inspiration ready-made from some heaven of perfections of which he knows nothing. And I would not grudge him the proud illusion that will come sometimes to a writer: the illusion that his achievement has almost equalled the greatness of his dream.

—Joseph Conrad

Imagination is more important than experience and inspiration. I don't want to give a faithful report on real-life incidents, I want to *transform* them in my imagination so that the story itself becomes the event; it isn't just an authentic report referring to something outside itself. When my son was a child, he didn't want me to *read* a story to him; he urged me to "make up a story." He wanted to experience the process itself, to feel my imagination at work inventing.

—DAVID MADDEN

Imagination is as necessary to a novelist or short-story writer as the spinning of webs is to a spider and just as mysterious. . . . Imagination cannot be created, but it can be fostered, and this fostering is part of the writer's duty. It is not enough to congratulate oneself on having been gifted (lovely word!) with imagination, though it is certainly a major cause for rejoicing. The imagination, like the intellect, has to be used, and a creative writer ought to exercise it all the time. There is no idea, however insignificant or vague it may be, that the imagination cannot touch to new beginnings, turning it around and around in different lights, playing with it, *listening* to it.

—B. J. CHUTE

(*See Creativity, Ideas, Imagery.*)

IMITATION

If you do not make the right beginning, you will never be able to write. They will put you down as one who has been influenced by another, and that will be the end. If they do that with your first stories, and your first book, there will never be any freedom from their judgment. The way not to write like anybody else in the

120

world is to go to the world itself, to life itself, to the senses of the living body itself, and to *translate* in your *own* way what you see, and hear, and smell, and taste, and feel, and imagine, and dream and do: *translate* the thing or the act or the thought or the mood into your own language. If you make the right beginning, nothing can stop you, and all you will have to do is survive.

> —WILLIAM SAROYAN, A Letter to a Talented Young Unpublished Writer

Artists, poets, writers, if you keep on copying others, no one will copy you.

> —JACQUES-HENRI BERNARDIN DE SAINT-PIERRE

You must learn by imitation. I could have been arrested for imitating Lardner in my pieces in the late 1920s—not the content, but the manner. These influences gradually fall away.

> —S. J. PERELMAN

Don't ever hesitate to imitate another writer—every artist learning his craft needs some models. Eventually you will find your own voice and shed the skin of the writer you imitated. But pick only the best models. If you want to write about medicine, read Lewis Thomas; if you want to write literary criticism, read Edmund Wilson and Alfred Kazin.

> —WILLIAM ZINSSER

(*See Originality.*)

IMPRESSIONS

If experience consists of impressions, it may be said that impressions *are* experience, just as (have we not seen it?) they are the very air we breathe. Therefore, if I should certainly say to a novice, "Write from experience and from experience only," I should feel that this was rather a tantalizing monition if I were not careful immediately to add, "Try to be one of the people on whom nothing is lost."

—HENRY JAMES

We accepted the name impressionists because we saw that life did not narrate but made impressions on our brains. We, in turn, if we wished to produce an effect of life, must not narrate but render impressions.

—FORD MADOX FORD

(*See Experience.*)

INCLUSIVENESS

Woe to the author determined to teach!
The best way to be boring is to leave nothing out.

—VOLTAIRE

(*See Boredom.*)

INFLUENCES

Young writers ought to find two or three authors in the last century who make them feel they knew what it was all about. And then try to figure out how they did it. Where style is concerned, I would go to as many movies and plays as I could, and read the words of people who are experimenting.

Look at the new people to figure out what they are into, and then decide virtues of your own and go to work. But I would certainly look at revolutionary and experimental forms in all fields: poetry, drama, painting, architecture, and then I'd move into the twenty-first century.

—JAMES MICHENER

In many European and American bookstores on the same shelves in which in the '60s were the works of Marx, Gramsci, Marcuse and Adorno, now there were books on the Age of Aquarius, on the New Age, on Indian philosophy, tarots and so on. After an excess of political and economic interpretation of life, the so-called radicalism or Marxism of the generation of '68, there has been a collapse of such Utopia, and many of these people went in search of something mysterious, supernatural and occult. There has been a turn of a whole generation, yearning for mystery, for revelation, for illumination.

—UMBERTO ECO

I had no other direction than my parents' taste for whatever was highest and best in literature; but I found out for myself many forgotten fields which proved the richest of pastures; and so far as a preference of a particular "style" is concerned, I believe mine was just the same at first as at last. I cannot name any one author who exclusively influenced me in that respect—as to the fittest expression of thought—but thought itself had many impulsions from very various sources.

—ROBERT BROWNING

Perhaps the nearest approach to a method I can lay claim to was a distinct aim at conciseness. After a while I received a hint from my sister that my love of conciseness tended to make my writing obscure, and I then endeavored to avoid obscurity as well as diffuseness. In poetics my elder brother was my acute and most helpful critic, and both prose and verse I used to read aloud to my dearest mother and my sister.

—CHRISTINA G. ROSSETTI

The book that had most to do with influencing me was Plutarch's *Lives;* and now, at the age of sixty [1887], when my will grows drowsy and my ambition begins to halt, I take to that book, and am well at once.

—GENERAL LEW WALLACE

What one reads doesn't influence one as much as where one is. Still, a great many writers have had their effect on me. The serious ones, I guess, were Ford Madox Ford, Joseph Conrad and Henry James. He was my idol, but to say he influenced me is a bit absurd—like saying a mountain influenced a mouse.

—GRAHAM GREENE

(*See Gurus, Reading As a Writer.*)

INSPIRATION

You have to be inspired to write something like [*Plutonium Ode*]. It's not something you can very easily do just by pressing a button. You have to have the right historical and physical combination, the right mental formation, the right courage, the right sense of prophecy, and the right information, intentions, and ambitions.

—ALLEN GINSBERG

Inspiration is wonderful when it happens, but the writer must develop an approach for the rest of the time. The approach must involve getting something down on the page: something good, mediocre or even bad. It is essential to the writing process that we unlearn all those seductive high school maxims about waiting for inspiration. The wait is simply too long.

—LEONARD S. BERNSTEIN

(*See Effort, Motivation, Self-Starting.*)

INTEGRITY

Look in thy heart and write.

—SIR PHILIP SIDNEY

Write till your ink be dry, and with your tears
Moist it again, and frame some feeling line
That may discover such integrity.

—WILLIAM SHAKESPEARE, *The*
Two Gentlemen of Verona, III, 2

On her best work: Nothing was really worth while that did not cut pretty deep . . . the main thing was always to be honest.

—WILLA CATHER

The most essential gift for a good writer is a built-in, shockproof shit detector. This is the writer's radar and all great writers have it.

—ERNEST HEMINGWAY

(*See Honesty, Truth.*)

INTEREST

The chief use of a plot is one that many people do not seem to have noticed. It is a line to direct the reader's interest. That is possibly the most important thing in fiction, for it is by direction of interest that the author carries the reader along from page to page and it is by direction of interest that he induces in him the mood that he desires. The author always loads his dice, but he must never let the reader see that he has done so, and by the manipulation of his plot, he can engage the reader's attention so that he does not perceive that violence has been done him.

—W. Somerset Maugham

My most important piece of advice to all you would-be writers: *when you write, try to leave out all the parts readers skip.*

—Elmore Leonard

(*See Boredom, Inclusiveness, Mood, Pace.*)

INTERPRETATION

I perceived that to . . . write that essential book, which is the only true one, a great writer does not, in the current meaning of the word, invent it, but, since it exists already in each one of us, interprets it. The duty and the task of a writer are those of an interpreter.

—Marcel Proust

I'm always, always trying to interpret Life in terms of lives, never just lives in terms of characters.

—Eugene O'Neill

(*See Contact with Reader, Duty to Reader.*)

INVOLVEMENT

Nothing I wrote saved a single Jew from being gassed . . . it's perfectly all right to be an *engagé* writer as long as you don't think you're changing things. Art is our chief means of breaking bread with the dead.

—W. H. AUDEN

To understand social reality, one must be inside it, participate in its movements and its struggles.

—IGNAZIO SILONE

(*See Human Rights, Literary Politics, Moral Position.*)

J

JOURNALISM

Afflict the comfortable and comfort the afflicted.

—JOURNALISTIC CREDO

My advice to young journalists is: Be a nuisance. Annoy the hell out of the city desk. You might get away with it.

—I. F. STONE

Ask how to live? Write, write, write anything. The world's a fine believing world, write news!

—JOHN FLETCHER (1614)

Advice for would-be sportswriters:
Loving sports would be the very least recommendation for someone who wants to be a sportswriter. First, he should really feel he wants to be a newspaperman. Then I would suggest he get as much formal education as possible, not necessarily in a school of journalism, but reading languages, philosophy, history, economics, sociology. Then go out and hound a city editor for a job and work

on the local side of the paper under the discipline of a city desk. Learn what the newspaper business is all about. After that, it's easy to get a transfer into sports.

—RED SMITH

"Write short dramatic leads to your stories," [James] Thurber's editor told him during his early days as a newspaper reporter. Soon after, he turned in a murder story that began:

Dead. That's what the man was when they found him with a knife in his back at 4 P.M. in front of Riley's saloon at the corner of 52nd and 12th Streets.

—ROBERT HENDRICKSON

Advice for beginning columnists:

Never put the story in the lead. Forget all that journalism-school stuff you drilled into your reporters; this new life is not straightline newspapering, it is hot-shot philosophizing. You do not have to pander to your readers' habits; let them get into your habit, which may include reading your column warily, wondering what your message really is. Let 'em have a hot shot of ambiguity right between the eyes.

As you cultivate the garden of controversy, burn the bridges of *objectivity.* Show me an evenhanded columnist and I'll show you an odds-on favorite soporific. What is required in a great editor and expected of a great reporter is death to a provocative pundit. . . . Keep 'em guessing, muttering, off balance. Even a jerk who knees is better than a knee that jerks. (That is one of those meaningless turnaround sentences that copy editors are trained to cut out as cutesy; Op-Ed copy editors are forced to leave them in, for fear of stifling a profundity.)

—WILLIAM SAFIRE

(*See Reporting.*)

JOURNALS

There is nothing too trifling to write down so it be in the least degree characteristic. You will be surprised to find on re-perusing your journal what an importance and graphic power these little particulars assume.

—NATHANIEL HAWTHORNE

JOY IN WRITING

Putting a book together is interesting and exhilarating. It is sufficiently difficult and complex that it engages all your intelligence. It is life at its most free. Your freedom as a writer is not freedom in the sense of wild blurting; you may not let rip. It is life at its most free, if you are fortunate enough to be able to try it, because you select your materials, invent your task, and pace yourself.

—ANNIE DILLARD

(*See Pride in Being a Writer.*)

JUDGMENT

The secret of all good writing is sound judgment.

—HORACE

K

KEY EVENT

If the writer has not determined his key event, or if the key event
is not truly a key, the structure of the story will be loose and vague,
the effect will be one of diffuseness, and the reader will be puzzled
rather than enlightened. We can examine any satisfactory story
and locate the key event, or the key moment. . . . Such a moment
brings into focus all previous events. It is the moment of illumination for the whole story. It is the germ of the story, and contains
in itself, by implication at least, the total meaning of the story.

—CLEANTH BROOKS and ROBERT
PENN WARREN

(*See Form, Structure.*)

L

LANGUAGE

Clear your mind of cant.

—SAMUEL JOHNSON

Never use a metaphor, simile or other figure of speech which
   you are used to seeing in print.
Never use a long word where a short one will do.
If it is possible to cut a word out, always cut it out.
Never use the passive where you can use the active.
Never use a foreign phrase, a scientific word or a jargon word if
   you can think of an everyday British equivalent.
Break any of these rules sooner than say anything outright bar-
   baric.

—GEORGE ORWELL

English is a stretch language; one size fits all. That does not mean
anything goes; in most instances, anything does not go. But the
language, as it changes, conforms itself to special groups and occasions: There is a time for dialect, a place for slang, an occasion
for literary form. What is correct on the sports page is out of place
on the Op-Ed page; what is with-it on the street may well be

without it in the classroom. The spoken language does not have the same standards as the written language—the tune you whistle is not the orchestra's score. Even profanity's acceptance changes; in the '30s, Clark Gable's line in *Gone With the Wind*—"Frankly, my dear, I don't give a damn"—was passed by the Hays office provided the actor placed the emphasis on "give" rather than "damn." Today, traditionalists would be happy to settle for an emphatic "damn" rather than an earthier expletive.

—WILLIAM SAFIRE

(*See Credos, Dialogue, Grammar, Slang.*)

LETTER WRITING

Care should be taken, not that the reader *may* understand, but that he *must* understand.

—QUINTILIAN

Let your letter be written as accurately as you are able—I mean as to language, grammar, and stops, but as to the matter of it the less trouble you give yourself the better it will be. Letters should be easy and natural, and convey to the persons to whom we send just what we would say if we were with them.

—LORD CHESTERFIELD

The first rule of all is to be prompt. This avoids having to write the kind of letter that starts with a long, boring (and probably incredible) explanation of why it took you so very long to write.

And a prompt answer is a sign that you genuinely care about the person you are writing to. When you put off writing too long, you are really telling someone "I've got more important things to think about than you."

When you do write, don't try for literary masterpieces. Write naturally, and say what you really feel—in the same words you would use in conversation. It's a mistake to think that words or expressions you know would sound stilted in person are somehow appropriate in a letter. They're not.

One final word: the warmest, wittiest letter in the world is a waste if your handwriting's not legible!

—Pamphlet from Crane's Fine
Papers company

A business letter must be:

Clear: Business cannot be conducted on guesswork.
Concise: A busy man has no time to waste on useless words.
Concrete: Abstract and general phrases blur the impression.

Don't use the headless forms: *Have sent . . . Enclose herewith . . . Beg to . . .* Courtesy and clearness demand: *We have sent . . . I enclose . . .* Never use the absurd *same,* as in the expression *we have shipped same . . .* Avoid such hackneyed and aimless phrases as *I would suggest . . . We beg to acknowledge your favor of . . . Please find enclosed . . .* Say: *I suggest that . . . We have your letter of . . . We enclose . . .*

—David Lambuth

LITERARY AGENTS

Get an agent. Make no excuses for the failure to do so. Get an agent. Otherwise you're a babe among wolves.

—Brendan Francis

LITERARY POLITICS

You know, for God's sake, fellas, let's get out and look at something for a change, and stop breathing the same ideas! Literary politics in this country has the whiff of people who work in these sealed buildings, where on Thursday you breathe the same air that went through all the lungs on Monday. It's really tiresome. That's where you get pernicious diseases, you know? Get out there! Take a look! Get involved in something!

—TOM WOLFE

(*See Human Rights, Influences, Moral Position.*)

LOVE INTEREST

Very much of a novelist's work must appertain to the intercourse between young men and young women. It is admitted that a novel can hardly be made interesting or successful without love. . . . It is necessary because the passion is one which interests or has interested all. Everyone feels it, has felt it, or expects to feel it—or else rejects it with an eagerness which still perpetuates the interest.

—ANTHONY TROLLOPE

LOVE SCENES

In writing love scenes, especially, trust your reader's imagination. I've written my share of extremely explicit scenes, but I believe my most memorable ones were those in which I focused on what my characters were feeling and thinking, rather than on what they were doing.

—JOAN DIAL

(*See Characterization, Sex.*)

M

MARGINAL NOTES

One should always lay aside the first draft for three or four weeks to give the conscious and subconscious mind time to think about it before beginning a revision. When the author does this, he will find himself making notes on the margins of some of the pages of the first draft on how to improve the work. . . . Here are a few examples of the marginal notes on the first draft of a novel that later became a best-seller:

> Faulty exposition. Rewrite.
> Scene drags. Cut it.
> Motivation weak. Make stronger.
> Kill this action scene. Put into narrative.
> Good scene. Build it up.
> Prose awkward. Rewrite.
> Protagonist's dialogue out of character. Rephrase.
> Chapter rambles and is overwritten. Tighten.
> Dialogue stiff. Rewrite.
> Faulty exposition. How would she know this? Rewrite.
> Lousy transition. Revise.
> Chance for big scene here. Change from narrative to action.

—ROBERT MEREDITH and JOHN FITZGERALD

(See Cutting, Drafts, Revision.)

MATURATION

I learned never to empty the well of my writing, but always to stop when there was still something there in the deep part of the well, and let it refill at night from the springs that fed it.

—ERNEST HEMINGWAY

You have to learn how to use your energy and not squander it. In the writing process, the more a thing cooks, the better. The brain works for you even when you are at rest. I find dreams particularly useful. I myself think a great deal before I go to sleep and the details sometimes unfold in the dream.

—DORIS LESSING

It began as a diary . . . little by little it began to turn itself into a story, by that mysterious process which I cannot explain, but which I recognize when it begins, and I go along with it out of a kind of curiosity, as if my mind which knows the facts is watching to see what my story-telling mind will finally make of them.

—KATHERINE ANNE PORTER

I have learned in my thirty-odd years of serious writing only one sure lesson: stories, like whiskey, must be allowed to mature in the cask.

—SEÁN O'FÁOLAIN

MEMOIRS

If I, a living witness, one who experienced those times, don't speak about them, then others who did not experience or witness these times will invent their own version of them.

—ANATOLY RYBAKOV

(See Autobiography, Confessions.)

MEMORY

If you wish to remember a thing well, put it in writing, even if you burn the paper immediately after you have done; for the eye greatly assists the mind. . . . Put down something every day in the year, if it be merely a description of the weather. You will not have done this for one year without finding the benefit of it. It disburthens the mind of many things to be recollected; it is amusing and useful, and ought by no means to be neglected.

—WILLIAM COBBETT

You have . . . notes in front of you; but let them spur, not drag you onward. In short, *write from memory*—as far as possible—with only occasional prompting from the notes, and make everything correct and shipshape later. Once you have "something down," as professional writers say, the job of verifying, improving, cutting, and polishing is pure pleasure. Unlike the sculptor, the writer can start carving and enjoying himself only after he has dug the marble out of his own head—pity the poor writer!

—JACQUES BARZUN

(*See Scene/Setting.*)

MESSAGE

We should continue to write in spite of the bruises and the vast silence that frequently surrounds us. A book is not an end in itself, it is only a way to touch someone—a bridge extended across a space of loneliness and obscurity—and sometimes it is a way of winning other people to our causes.

—ISABEL ALLENDE

[W. Somerset] Maugham said that he intended *Of Human Bondage* to be one long telegram to the reader.

—CHARLES MCCARRY

"But Mr. Goldwyn," a colleague asked at a script conference, "what is the *message* of this film?"

"I am just planning a movie," he replied. "I am not interested in messages. Messages are for Western Union."

—SAMUEL GOLDWYN

I get so sick of writers who make tedious demands on their readers and expect them to bear with them through infinitely refined analyses of meaning and this, that and the other. You really must have a story and you must tell it, or people will just put the book down and they will find it to be one of those books (unlike the ones you sometimes read about in book reviews) that once put down is impossible to take up again.

—ROBERTSON DAVIES

(*See Boredom, Moral Position, Pedantry, Political Writing, Theme.*)

METAPHOR

The greatest thing in style is to have a command of metaphor.

—ARISTOTLE

The writer Robert Penn Warren tells about a student who had written a nice short story, which Warren praised. The young man said, "Oh, it's not finished yet. I have to go back and put in some symbols." Don't think your writing is unfinished if it doesn't have images and metaphors. Images and metaphors will come into your writing when they need to as unavoidably as symbols come into fiction.

—BILL STOUT

Aristotle rightly chose, as the prime mark of a poet, the craft of metaphor—a gift for discovering in the world and then for transmitting clearly a stream of likeness in visible nature. A glance at any page of [Eudora] Welty's fiction is likely to show more than one such yoking of disparate sights in a single image of startling freshness:

His memory could work like the slinging of a noose to catch a wild pony.

—REYNOLDS PRICE

Beware of the metaphor. It is the spirit of good prose. It gives the reader a picture, a glimpse of what the subject really looks like to the writer. But it is dangerous, can easily get tangled and insistent, the more so when it almost works: don't have a violent explosion pave the way for a new growth.

—SHERIDAN BAKER

Metaphors should not be used in such close association with unmetaphorical language as to produce absurdity or confusion.
The principle is best illustrated by this short sentence from a melodramatic chapter in Graham Greene's novel *It's a Battlefield:*

Kay Rummer sat with her head in her hands and her eyes on the floor.

And her teeth on the mantelpiece? A slip like this will break the spell of a novel for any intelligent reader.

—Robert Graves and Alan
Hodge

(See Figurative Expression.)

METHOD

"It's very unsophisticated," he [Irving Wallace] replied, "and I only work on one book at a time." He explained that when he got ideas, he wrote them down in pencil and filed them away. He also said he strongly believed in organizing his novels before he began to write them.

—Richard Severo

There is no method except to be very intelligent.

—T. S. Eliot

You have to throw yourself away when you write.

—Maxwell Perkins

All those who I think have lived as literary men will agree with me that three hours a day will produce as much as a man ought to write. . . . It had at this time become my custom—and it still is my custom, though of late I have become a little lenient to myself—to write with my watch before me, and to require from myself 250 words every quarter of an hour.

—Anthony Trollope

I put a piece of paper under my pillow and when I could not sleep I wrote in the dark.

—HENRY DAVID THOREAU

A possibly apocryphal story has it that Voltaire did at least some of his writing in bed, using his naked mistress's back as a desk.

—ROBERT HENDRICKSON

(*See Discipline, Environment, Solitude, Work Process, Work Station.*)

MINIMALISM

The trouble with minimalists is that they have anomie, ennui and despair, which we all have (we older writers have much more cause for it), but they refuse to allow the richness of life, of the universe. The universe is alive, teeming with things . . . they leave all that out of their work. . . . There is a lot outside of us, and they just won't put it in. . . . I don't like what they have done to literature because they have produced a generation of readers who are bound by their own skin. . . . From me to me. Where is it going to take you? There is something else out there. Matthew Arnold said that "literature is a criticism of life," which I still believe.

—LYNN SHARON SCHWARTZ

George Garrett says, "Minimalism is always less than meets the eye." No, it's not. Jokes and fairy tales, the moon and sand dunes, Mondrian and Chinese vases are pretty good. A friend and I once stood in front of the glass case of Cycladic sculptures at the Met and she said, "It makes you proud to be a human being." Rap bad,

142

dumb, derivative minimalism and bad, dumb baroque, which has so much more to be about less with.

—LORE SEGAL

Stanley Elkin, no lover of those writers he has called "the Minimalistas," when advised by an editor that "less is more," retorted, "I don't believe less is more. I believe that more is more. I believe that less is less, fat fat, thin thin and enough is enough."

—KEN EMERSON

MISTAKES

Spelling mistakes, typos, mistakes in idiom, unfashionable usages, all these characterize you as a writer controlled by language rather than controlling it. You present yourself as still in rompers. It is not a question of being *clear*. These revelations of self don't usually obscure ideas, they obscure you. They reveal that you have not paid attention to your own writing and invite the reader to respond in kind.

—RICHARD A. LANHAM

MOMENTUM

When my horse is running good, I don't stop to give him sugar.

—WILLIAM FAULKNER

. . . the heat of writing. I call it heat not because one does or should write in a fever, but because the deliberate choice of words and

143

links and transitions is easiest and best when it is made from a throng of ideas bubbling under the surface of consciousness. On this account, I strongly recommend writing ahead full tilt, not stopping to correct. Cross out no more than the few words that will permit you to go on when you foresee a blind alley. Leave some words in blank, some sentences not complete. Keep going!

—JACQUES BARZUN

Once you commit yourself to moving forward, you can't stop. It goes back to the metaphor of the miler going back to rerun a last quarter mile because he didn't do his best job. You can't do it! To understand the rhythm of writing a hundred pages you have to write right through. Feel the pages under you the same way a runner feels the gravel under his feet. He can tell how fast that gravel is moving under his feet as he's going a mile, the same way you can tell how fast the pages are, how fast the scenes are moving. . . . I believe the script should read and feel *fast*.

—PAUL SCHRADER

(*See Boredom, Pace, Putting It Off, Second Wind.*)

MOOD

Another choice is unity of mood. You might want to talk to the reader in the casual and chatty voice that *The New Yorker* has so strenuously refined. Or you might want to approach him with a certain formality to describe a serious event or to acquaint him with a set of important facts. Both tones are acceptable. In fact, any tone is acceptable. But don't mix two or three.

—WILLIAM ZINSSER

If the writer's purpose is to communicate a mood, he succeeds better by re-creating the object as he sees it. A writer who tells us he is afraid does not necessarily frighten us; but if he can throw before us the fearsome thing in all its horror, he probably will. In practice, however, impressionistic description uses both methods, often employing direct statement of mood as a center about which to organize the more precise details of indirect description.

—THOMAS S. KANE and LEONARD
J. PETERS

(*See Essay, Tone.*)

MORAL POSITION

Every work of art adheres to some system of morality. But if it be really a work of art, it must contain the essential criticism of the morality to which it adheres.

—D. H. LAWRENCE

A writer who does not passionately believe in the perfectability of man has no dedication nor any membership in literature.

—JOHN STEINBECK

A novelist has to take a reading of the world, and that is what happens in all the novels that interest me. Just what is going on here? It sounds banal, but it's an absolutely vital question for the novelist. It's the highest investigation. . . . Style is not neutral; it gives moral directions.

—MARTIN AMIS

Concern with morality makes every work of the imagination false and stupid.

—GUSTAVE FLAUBERT

Avoid any moral affectation; people don't look for this in the novel. If the characters required for your project are occasionally compelled to reason, may this always be unaffected and without any pretension. The author should never moralize, only the character, and only allow him to do this when circumstances force him.

—MARQUIS DE SADE

Shakespeare with his excellencies has likewise faults. . . . He sacrifices virtue to convenience, and is so much more careful to please than to instruct, that he seems to write without any moral purpose. . . . He makes no just distribution of good or evil. . . . He carries his persons indifferently through right and wrong. . . . This fault the barbarity of his age cannot extenuate, for it is always a writer's duty to make the world better, and justice is a virtue independent of time or place.

—SAMUEL JOHNSON

Think no evil, see no evil, hear no evil—and you will never write a best-selling novel.

—DAN BENNETT

Your business as a writer is not to illustrate virtue but to show how a fellow may move toward it or away from it.

—ROBERT PENN WARREN

Writers and artists . . . can vanquish lies! In the struggle against lies, art has always won and always will. Lies can stand up against much of the world but not against art.

—ALEXANDER I. SOLZHENITSYN

The storyteller asks questions that are seldom completely resolved. Tolstoy does not prove anything about the nature of love in *Anna Karenina,* but he opens up new questions for the reader. Chaim Potok does not prove the existence of God, but his own strong awareness of God permeates his novels. The true storyteller does not, in fact, have to prove anything. The storyteller has to tell a good story.

—MALCOLM L'ENGLE

To me a writer is one of the most important soldiers in the fight for the survival of the human race. He must stay at his post in the thick of fire to serve the cause of mankind.

—LEON URIS

The task which the artist implicitly sets himself is to overthrow existing values, to make of the chaos around him an order which is his own, to sow strife and ferment so that by the emotional release those who are dead may be restored to life.

—HENRY MILLER

(*See Good vs. Evil, Human Rights, Involvement, Message, Theme.*)

MOTIVATION

You don't write because you want to say something; you write because you've got something to say.

—F. Scott Fitzgerald

All this advice from senior writers to establish a discipline—always to get down a thousand words a day whatever one's mood—I find an absurdly puritanical and impractical approach. Write, if you must, because you feel like writing, never because you feel you *ought* to write.

—John Fowles

One writes to make a home for oneself, on paper, in time and in others' minds.

—Alfred Kazin

[The writer] must essentially draw from life as he sees it, lives it, overhears it or steals it, and the truer the writer, perhaps the bigger the blackguard. He lives by biting the hand that feeds him.

—Charles Jackson

You may ask what will set the caldron of ideas bubbling. *Wanting to tell* is the answer. . . . There must also be something to be told, of which you have the secret. . . . Make believe that you want to bring somebody around to your opinion; in other words, adopt a thesis and start expounding. Or else, imagine the need to instruct someone in a piece of learning you possess. . . . With a slight effort

148

of this kind at the start—a challenge to utterance—you will find your pretense disappearing and a real concern creeping in. The subject will have taken hold of you as it does in the work of all habitual writers.

—JACQUES BARZUN

I want to make a book and a kid, because they are the only ways to overcome death, a paper thing and a flesh thing. Lovemaking alone, for all its pleasures, is stupid; nothing comes of it. But my death can have a sense if somebody survives me and continues. And I write a book, not to have a success now but with the hope that in the next millennium, it will be still at least in a bibliography or in a footnote. And if I like the success now, it's because probably it helps the book to survive.

—UMBERTO ECO

When you're writing, you're trying to find out something which you don't know. The whole language of writing for me is finding out what you don't want to know, what you don't want to find out. But something forces you to anyway.

—JAMES BALDWIN

Always dream and shoot higher than you know you can do. Don't bother just to be better than your contemporaries or predecessors. Try to be better than yourself. An artist is a creature driven by demons. He doesn't know why they choose him and he's usually too busy to wonder why. He is completely amoral in that he will rob, borrow, beg, or steal from anybody and everybody to get the work done. The writer's only responsibility is to his art.

—WILLIAM FAULKNER

If you would not be forgotten as soon as you are dead, either write things worth reading or do things worth writing.

—BENJAMIN FRANKLIN

The big motivation for me was the desire to be independent, to get up when you want, write what you want and work where you want.

—IRVING WALLACE

Motivation means *what-do-they-want-and-why?* With strong motivation, you'll have strong conflict. Your main character, first of all, should be striving for some life-or-death issue. Perhaps literally; perhaps only because happiness is at stake. In the long run, happiness is always at stake.

—PHYLLIS A. WHITNEY

(*See Effort, Inspiration, Moral Position, Self-Starting, Subject.*)

MYSTERY/DETECTIVE

Rules of the classic mystery:

There must be a crime and it must be personalized to the point where the reader cares.

The criminal must appear reasonably early in the story. . . . The villain of the piece must be evident for a goodly portion of the book.

The author must be rigorously honest, and all clues, whether physical, such as a fingerprint or a dropped purple bandanna, a character trait, or an emotional relationship between people, must be made available to the reader.

The detective must exert effort to catch the criminal, and the criminal must exert effort to fool the detective and escape from him.

—LAWRENCE TREAT

To stir the reader is the writer's whole purpose. It is he who turns the mirror to the proper angle—for his own enlightenment, as well as the enlightenment of future generations. Remember that it is not crime or the fact of evil that is important to the mystery writer, but the way we, as artists, view evil and what we do about it.

—BRUCE CASSIDAY

I seat myself at the typewriter and hope, and lurk. When an idea appears, I leap on it with all fours and hold it down till I've mastered it. Ideally, I start at the wrong end, the finale. Then I try to develop strong conflicts and use the murder of a catalyst character. I just loathe it when an author has to force a murderer to confess. I always try to evolve jury evidence; it's one of the demands I make on myself: the dénouement must be incontrovertible *evidence* that a district attorney can use. And I want to tell a good story, like a juggler, keep the balls soaring in the air and hope the reader's eyes stay on them; be fair and give clues to the puzzle.

—MIGNON EBERHART

Stripped of its decorations and embellishments, the detective story is at bottom one thing only: a conflict of wits between criminal and sleuth, in which the detective is traditionally victorious by outthinking his adversary. Each important plot incident, every structural step of the story, must be the perfect and logical consequence and result of this central conflict of crime and pursuit, just as each move in a chess game determines and is determined by a counter move. The formula is capable of infinite variations, as in chess. It may be adorned and disguised in almost any fashion the author chooses, whether gaudy or sober. But in basic structure it must never vary by so much as a hairsbreadth from absolute logicality. Beside this one simple rule, all other rules pale to relative unimportance. This is the detective story.

—HOWARD HAYCRAFT

What is your destination, or the *target* of your book? Many writers, especially mystery writers, actually write the endings to their books *first*. Your ending may prove a useful starting point in fine-tuning your focus.

—KATHLEEN KRULL

N

NAMES

You don't want a name that jars, however slightly, every time it appears on the page, unless that is your intent. Heroines do not have to have musical names such as Roxanne, Stephanie, Tiffany or Michele. By the same token, avoid such model-perfect names as Darien or Sean. . . . In choosing names, it is easy to fall back on stereotypes. You should research the names of characters carefully, according to their ages, the region of the country where they live, and their nationality, but avoid naming them exactly what your reader would expect. . . . Keep your characters' ages in mind when you write. Someday there may be a lot of grandmothers named Lisa or Kim, but not right now.

—PHYLLIS REYNOLDS NAYLOR

Give your characters interesting names. Names can define a character. They can also function ironically and humorously. . . . Big Daddy in Tennessee Williams' *Cat on a Hot Tin Roof* is the head of a wealthy household, and not only does he command obedience and servitude, but the humorous overtones of his name add an ironic dimension.

—LAVONNE MUELLER

NEW WRITERS

If I were to advise new writers, if I were to advise the new writer in myself, going into the theatre of the Absurd, the almost-Absurd, the theatre of Ideas, the any-kind-of-theatre-at-all, I would advise like this:

Tell me no pointless jokes.
I will laugh at your refusal to allow me laughter.

Build in me no tension toward tears and refuse me my lamentations.
I will go find me better wailing walls.

Do not clench my fists for me and hide the target.
I might strike you, instead.

Above all, sicken me not unless you show me the way to the ship's rail. For, please understand, if you poison me, I must be sick. It seems to me that many people writing the sick film, the sick novel, the sick play, have forgotten that poison can destroy minds.

—RAY BRADBURY

(See Aim, Purpose.)

NONFICTION: THEMES

Leading all themes is the fight to survive. People want to read about this whether it concerns the survival of a man, a mouse, or a worm. The second most demanded theme is man's ability, in William Faulkner's words, not only to survive but to prevail. Another successful theme is how to prevail and to be happy at the same time. How to be and how to do are almost certain guarantees of a successful book or article: how to be beautiful, happy, popular, healthy, strong, successful (socially, sexually, professionally, spiritually) and how to do anything from subdividing a tiny planeria to visiting another planet. Still another popular theme is lifting the veil of mystery, going behind the scenes and observing how other people live, prevail, and die.

—ISABELLE ZIEGLER

Choice of subject is of cardinal importance. One does by far one's best work when besotted by and absorbed in the matter at hand.

—JESSICA MITFORD

(*See Theme.*)

NOVELS

The business of the novelist is not to relate great events, but to make small ones interesting.

—ARTHUR SCHOPENHAUER

The novel remains for me one of the few forms where we can record man's complexity and the strength and decency of his longings. Where we can describe, step by step, minute by minute, our not altogether unpleasant struggle to put ourselves into a viable and devout relationship to our beloved and mistaken world.

—JOHN CHEEVER

O

OBJECTIVITY

To a chemist nothing on earth is unclean. A writer must be as objective as a chemist; he must abandon the subjective line; he must know that dung-heaps play a very respectable part in a land-scape, and that evil passions are as inherent in life as good ones.

—Anton Chekhov

When a writer knows home in his heart, his heart must remain subtly apart from it. He must always be a stranger to the place he loves, and its people.

—Willie Morris

Every scene, even the commonest, is wonderful, if only one can detach oneself, casting off all memory of use and custom, and behold it (as it were) for the first time; in its right, authentic colours; without making comparisons. The novelist should cherish and burnish this faculty of seeing crudely, simply, artlessly, igno-rantly; of seeing like a baby or a lunatic, who lives each moment by itself and tarnishes by the present no remembrance of the past.

—Arnold Bennett

I have found that a story leaves a deeper impression when it is impossible to tell which side the author is on.

—LEO TOLSTOY

The artist must work with indifference—too great interest vitiates his work.

—HENRY DAVID THOREAU

(*See Emotion, Moral Position, Omniscient Authors, Point of View.*)

OBSCURITY

Let the readers do some of the work themselves.

—FYODOR DOSTOYEVSKY,
defending his right to produce
books that were difficult and
intricate

A story should be managed so that it should *suggest* interesting things to the *reader* instead of the author's doing all the thinking for him, and setting it before him in black and white.

—SARAH ORNE JEWETT

The form of sincere poetry, unlike the form of the popular poetry, may indeed be sometimes obscure, or ungrammatical as in some of the best of the Songs of Innocence and Experience, but it must have the perfections that escape analysis, the subtleties that have a new meaning every day, and it must have all this whether it be but

157

a little song made out of a moment of dreamy indolence, or some great epic made out of the dreams of one poet and of a hundred generations whose hands were never weary of the sword.

—W. B. YEATS

Art is not difficult because it wishes to be difficult, rather because it wishes to be art. However much the writer might long to be straightforward, these virtues are no longer available to him. He discovers that in being simple, honest, straightforward, nothing much happens.

—DONALD BARTHELME, rebutting
criticism of himself and of other
writers as being too difficult

I don't think that the reader of the book should know the exact meaning of everything. Suppose I am a film maker and I show you a character walking in the dark in a castle holding only a candle, and you come to ask me: "Would you put a lamp on the scene to illuminate it?" But why? If I wanted the scene to be dark it's because that darkness has a meaning.

—UMBERTO ECO

Kafka . . . constructs a kind of labyrinth where the logic is perfect, but it leads you into areas that are completely unexpected, such that you think you're going one way and then you wind up in the other direction. And I've found that when you're composing a work, it's exactly the same—you don't want to know at the outset where you'll be at the end of the scene. You have a vague idea, of course, but it's not a matter of going in a straight line, you have all kinds of divagations. . . . What I want most to create is a kind of deceiving transparency, as if you are looking in very transparent water and can't make an estimation of the depths.

—PIERRE BOULEZ

158

Just as the writer cannot give the total past in his exposition, so he cannot give the total present in his scene. His problem is to select the relevant details, the items which will suggest the whole scene, and in certain cases give clues to character, situation and theme. Chekhov once told a writer to cut out his long passage describing the moonlight in a scene and give simply the glint of the moon on a piece of broken bottle.

—CLEANTH BROOKS and ROBERT PENN WARREN

(*See Complexity, Subtlety.*)

OBSERVATION

The first secret of good writing: We must look *intently,* and hear *intently,* and taste *intently* . . . we must look at everything *very hard.* Is it the task at hand to describe a snowfall? Very well. We begin by observing that the snow is white. Is it as white as bond paper? White as whipped cream? Is the snow daisy white, or egg-white white, or whitewash white? Let us look very hard. We will see that snow comes in different textures. The light snow that looks like powdered sugar is not the heavy snow that clings like wet cotton. When we write matter-of-factly that *Last night it snowed and this morning the fields were white,* we have not looked *intently.* Out of this intensity of observation we derive two important gains. We learn to write precisely; and we fill our storehouse with the images that one day we will fashion into similes and metaphors.

—JAMES J. KILPATRICK

This is a period of thresholds, of tremendous changes, as we come to the end of certain experiments, and as new people come to this country from all over the place. This is an amazing, wonderful period in which to be a writer. I don't see how a writer can operate without going out as a reporter. I don't care if you're writing plays, movies, or even if you're a poet—I don't see any other way to do it. And yet so many writers are at this moment turning inward. I don't get it! Think of the feast that's out there.

—Tom Wolfe

(*See Details, Precision, Reporting.*)

OFFENSIVENESS

In this century if we are not willing to risk giving offense, we have no claim to the title of artists, and if we are not willing to face the possibility of being ourselves revised, offended, and changed by a work of art, we should leave the book unopened, the picture unviewed, and the symphony unheard.

—John Updike

To write with great restraint is to write dishonestly. To write effectively, a writer must be ready to spill a certain amount of blood on the sidewalk. . . . Not everyone has to stick with his whole life as closely as Thomas Wolfe did in *Look Homeward, Angel.* Sinclair Lewis's autobiographical *Main Street* prompted his whole hometown to hate him, sue him, and throw figurative rocks at him until he died, and then they erected monuments in his honor.

—Judy Delton

(*See Hurt Feelings.*)

OMISSION

If it is any use to know it, I always try to write on the principle of the iceberg. There is seven-eighths of it under water for every part that shows. Anything you know, you can eliminate and it only strengthens your iceberg. It is the part that doesn't show. If a writer omits something because he does not know it, then there is a hole in the story.

—Ernest Hemingway

The writer who cannot sometimes throw away a thought about which another man would have written dissertations, without worrying whether or not the reader will find it, will never become a great writer.

—Georg Christoph Lichtenberg

If a writer of prose knows enough about what he is writing about he may omit things that he knows and the reader, if the writer is writing truly enough, will have a feeling of those things as strongly as though the writer had stated them.

—Ernest Hemingway

(*See Inclusiveness.*)

OMNISCIENT AUTHORS

Madame Bovary has nothing true in it. It is a *totally fictitious* story; I put nothing in it of my own feelings or my own life. The illusion (if there is one) stems, on the contrary, from the *impersonality* of the book. This is one of my principles; you must not write *of yourself*. The artist must be within his work like God within the Creation; invisible and all-powerful; we feel him throughout, but we do not see him.

—Gustave Flaubert

(*See Objectivity, Point of View.*)

OPENINGS

Don't start by trying to make the book chronological. Just take a period. Then try to remember it so clearly that you can see things: what colors and how warm or cold or how you got there. Then try to remember people. And then just tell what happened. It is important to tell what people looked like, how they walked, what they wore, what they are. Put it all in. Don't try to organize it. And put in all the details you can remember. You will find that in a very short time things will begin to come back to you [that] you thought you had forgotten. Do it for very short periods at first but kind of think you aren't doing it.

> —JOHN STEINBECK, advising
> comedian Fred Allen how to
> write a novel

The point of attack should start your story. A story and especially a play must open with a crisis which is the sole point of attack—in the life or lives of one or more of the characters. A decision must be imminent and the characters must be ready to take action. . . . If you wish to write a good short story or novel, start on a note of crisis. No law states that you cannot start your story in any other way. But if you want to catch the reader's interest *immediately,* you had better start with a conflict.

> —LAJOS EGRI

A writer doesn't so much choose a story as a story chooses him. I know lots of stories, but for some reason only a few grab hold of me. They catch me and worry me and stick with me and raise questions for which I can't quite find answers. I start a novel from a real event or real people and make up characters along the way.

> —ROBERT PENN WARREN

We all know that the opening sentence of a commercial story must "hook" a reader. . . . Some literary stories, too, use the hook. Franz Kafka opened *The Metamorphosis* with: "As Gregor Samsa awoke one morning from uneasy dreams he found himself transformed in his bed into a gigantic insect." . . . To evaluate your own opening, it may help to analyze the beginning paragraphs of a wide range of stories and novels of varying types and quality.

—DAVID MADDEN

A mistake most people make, in my opinion, when they consider working on feature films, is that they feel like they have to get right into the action. I can promise you, in feature films you don't have to do that. It's more effective if you can get an audience to care about somebody before you throw 'em into an action sequence.

—LARRY FERGUSON

Find a subject you care about and which you in your heart feel others should care about. It is this genuine caring, not your games with language, which will be the most compelling and seductive element in your style.

—KURT VONNEGUT

(*See Beginning.*)

ORIGINALITY

The most original thing a writer can do is write like himself. It is also his most difficult task.

—ROBERTSON DAVIES

A work of art is individual; you cannot build it out of clichés, plastic, musical or verbal; it must be freshly thought and felt; it must spring from your own authentic seeing; it may be a poor thing, but if it is art, it must be your own. The work of every true artist is saturated with idiosyncrasy. "Art," said Zola, "is nature seen through a temperament." Who could confuse an El Greco with a Rubens, a Holbein, or a Whistler?

—Brand Blanchard

The most original modern authors are not so because they advance what is new, but simply because they know how to put what they have to say, as if it had never been said before.

—Goethe

Make it new.

—Ezra Pound

We need new art forms. New forms are wanted and if they aren't available, we might as well have nothing at all.

—Anton Chekhov

Whoever wants to be creative in good and evil, he must first be an annihilator and destroy values.

—Friedrich Nietzsche

Write it as it is, don't try to make it like this or that. You can't do it in anybody else's way—you will have to make a way of your own. If the way happens to be new, don't let that frighten you. Don't try to write the kind of short story that this or that magazine wants—write the truth, and let them take it or leave it.

—SARAH ORNE JEWETT to Willa
Cather

Every great and original writer, in proportion as he is great and original, must himself create the taste by which he is to be relished.

—WILLIAM WORDSWORTH

I owe all my originality, such as it is, to my determination not to be a literary man. Instead of belonging to a literary club I belong to a municipal council. Instead of drinking and discussing authors and reviews, I sit on committees with capable practical greengrocers and bootmakers (including a builder who actually reads Carlyle) and administer the collection of dust, the electric lighting of the streets, and the enforcement of the sanitary laws. You must do the same. Keep away from books and from men who get their ideas from books, and your own books will always be fresh.

—GEORGE BERNARD SHAW

The writer must always find expression for something which has never yet been expressed, must master a new set of phenomena which has never yet been mastered.

—EDMUND WILSON

It is better to fail in originality, than to succeed in imitation.

—HERMAN MELVILLE

(*See Brainstorming, Creativity, Ideas, Imagination, Imitation.*)

OUTLINING

The only good piece of advice that I ever read about playwriting was from John Van Druten, who said, "Don't outline everything, because it makes the writing of the play a chore." In other words, the fun and discovery are already gone . . . and now you've just got to write it out. Some writers *must* blueprint, but I would find it a chore to do that and then just try to dialogue it. I'm in the middle of a new play now—got about two-thirds of it done—and I don't know *exactly* how it's going to end, but I know I'll get it, and if one ending doesn't work, I'll just keep writing until I get it. They're all like big jigsaw puzzles, and that's what the fun of it is. You just keep looking around for the pieces.

—Neil Simon

When you write a novel, start with a plan—a careful plot outline, some notes to yourself on characters and settings, particular important events, and implications of meaning. In my experience, many young writers hate this step; they'd rather just plunge in. That's O.K., up to a point, but sooner or later the writer has no choice but to figure out what he's doing. Consider doing for yourself what movie people call a "treatment," a short narrative telling the whole story, introducing all the characters and events but skipping most of the particulars, including dialogue.

—John Gardner

The best time for planning a book is while you're doing the dishes.

—Agatha Christie

Planning to write is not writing. Outlining . . . researching . . .

166

talking to people about what you're doing, none of that is writing. Writing is writing.

—E. L. DOCTOROW

(*See Drafts, Marginal Notes, Planning, Revision.*)

OVERTONES

A great storyteller is never just a sort of out-of-work actor who has nothing else to do. He is somebody for whom storytelling is a vocation, a vocation that is related to his search through life. It is an act of devotion for him. Now, that doesn't make him tell a story in any pretentious or holy way. But it means that in the moment of *telling,* he is listening, with all that he has in him, to the *overtones* of the story, rather than stopping at the face value of the tale.

—PETER BROOK

P

PACE

There should be two main objectives in ordinary prose writing: to convey a message and to include in it nothing that will distract the reader's attention or check his habitual pace of reading—he should feel that he is seated at ease in a taxi, not riding a temperamental horse through traffic.

—ROBERT GRAVES and ALAN HODGE

Every scene you write can be more or less interesting depending on how you write it. Not every scene deserves full treatment, and there will be times when you'll hurry things along by summarizing a scene in a couple of sentences. But the more space you give to a scene and the more importance you assign to it, the greater is your obligation to make that scene pull its weight by commanding the reader's attention and keeping him interested and entertained.

—LAWRENCE BLOCK

A book should not be paced according to cinematic style. The pacing grows out of the subject matter of the book. If you're writing a psychological horror novel, the pacing should be slow, contemplative. If you're writing a novel about slasher killers, it should be a fast and hard-hitting pace.

—JAMES KISNER

(*See Boredom, Momentum, Scene/Setting.*)

PARAGRAPH

No one can say how long a paragraph should be. Subject, purpose, audience, editorial fashion, and individual preference, all affect the length and complexity of paragraphs. As a rough rule of thumb, however, you might think of expository paragraphs in terms of 120 or 150 words. . . . Numerous brief paragraphs are liable to be disjointed and underdeveloped. Great long ones fatigue readers. But remember—we are talking a very broad average. An occasional short paragraph of 15 to 20 words may work very well; so may an occasional long one of 300.

—THOMAS S. KANE

PASSION

Be still when you have nothing to say; when genuine passion moves you, say what you've got to say, and say it hot.

—D. H. LAWRENCE

Technique alone is never enough. You have to have passion. Technique alone is just an embroidered potboiler.

—RAYMOND CHANDLER

PEDANTRY

There is no need for the writer of fiction to be an expert of any subject but his own; on the contrary, it is hurtful to him, since, human nature being weak, he is hard put to it to resist the temptation of inappositely using his special knowledge. The novelist is ill-advised to be too technical. . . . The novelist should know something about the great issues that occupy men, who are his topics, but it is generally enough if he knows a little. He must avoid pedantry at all costs.

—W. SOMERSET MAUGHAM

(*See Message.*)

PERFECTIONISM

Don't be a perfectionist! That's what they tell you. It's impractical. We let adoration of compromise front for the stupidities that make compromise necessary. We say "Let's make the best of it" but we mean the easiest. The best is perfection. Perfectionists created the atomic bomb and a perfectionist created the "Ode on a Grecian Urn." If we must put up with less, let it growl and hiss in our acid gizzards as something we hate very much every day in the week.

—THOMAS HORNSBY FERRIL

PERSISTENCE

Go on writing plays, my boy. One of these days one of these London producers will go into his office and say to his secretary, "Is there a play from Shaw this morning?" and when she says

"No," he will say, "Well then, we have to start on the rubbish," and that's your chance, my boy.

—GEORGE BERNARD SHAW

(See Dedication, Discipline, Doggedness, Effect.)

PERSPECTIVE

To write is in some way to cut the seemingly automatic pattern of violence, destructiveness and death wish. To write is to put the seeming insignificance of human existence into a different perspective. It is the need, the wish, and please God, the ability, to reorder our physical faith.

—ALFRED KAZIN

Never write about a place until you're away from it, because that gives you perspective. Immediately after you've seen something you can give a photographic description of it and make it accurate. That's good practice, but it isn't creative writing.

—ERNEST HEMINGWAY

(See Pride in Being a Writer, Theme, Vision.)

PLAGIARISM

There is probably some long-standing "rule" among writers, journalists, and other word-mongers that says: "When you start stealing from your own work you're in bad trouble." And it may be true.

—HUNTER S. THOMPSON

There is no sixth commandment in art. The poet is entitled to lay his hands on whatever material he finds necessary for his work.

—HEINRICH HEINE

Keep your hands from literary picking and stealing. But if you cannot refrain from this kind of stealth, abstain from murdering what you steal.

—AUGUSTUS MONTAGUE TOPLADY

Great literature must spring from an upheaval in the author's soul. If that upheaval is not present, then it must come from the works of any other author which happen to be handy and easily adapted.

—ROBERT BENCHLEY

The beginning author ought to avoid plagiarizing the work of others—not on moral grounds, but simply because it will retard the development of his own faculties.

—JACK WOODFORD

PLANNING

You've chosen a subject (or had one chosen for you), explored it, thought about the topics you've discovered, gathered information about them. Now what? Are you ready to begin writing? Well, yes. But first you need a plan. Perhaps nothing more than a loose sense of purpose, held in your mind and never written down—what jazz musicians call a head arrangement. . . . But sometimes all of us (and most times most of us) require a more tangible plan. One kind is a statement of purpose: another is a preliminary, scratch outline.

—Thomas S. Kane

I write the first sentence and trust in God for the next.

—Laurence Sterne

There are all sorts of middle courses for novelists, but I am trying to suggest the two extremes. The second, that of Sterne and Giraudoux, implies a great deal of self-confidence, or trust in God. Even when followed by men of talent it is likely to produce formless, wasteful, inconsistent books, but the stories will flow like rivers or music and the characters may be a continual surprise to the author as well as the reader. The other method, that of the new fictionists, involves so much planning and preparation that the stories are no longer free to develop as in life. At best the stories will have an architectural form; their music is frozen and has ceased to flow; their economic structure is balanced in repose.

—Malcolm Cowley

When I start a book I have no idea of how it's going to end. I really don't know what's going to happen more than a chapter or two ahead. The characters audition in their opening scene—I listen to them, see how they sound. The plots develop on their own. If I'm curious enough to turn the pages, I figure it will have the same effect on readers.

—Elmore Leonard

(See Drafts, Outlining.)

PLAYWRITING

NINA: Your play's hard to act, there are no living people in it.
TREPLEV: Living people! We should show life neither as it is nor as it ought to be, but as we see it in our dreams.

—ANTON CHEKHOV
The Seagull, Act I

The critics still want me to be a poetic realist and I never was. All my *great* characters are larger than life, not realistic. In order to capture the quality of life in two and a half hours, everything has to be concentrated, intensified. You must catch life in moments of crisis, moments of electric confrontation. In reality, life is very *slow.* Onstage, you have only from 8:40 to 11:05 to get a lifetime of living across.

—TENNESSEE WILLIAMS

The playwright of today must dig at the roots of the sickness of today as he feels it—the death of the old God and the failure of science and materialism to give any satisfactory new one for the surviving primitive, religious instinct to find a meaning for life in, and to comfort its fears of death with.

—EUGENE O'NEILL

The theatre remains a place for language, a place to be *talked* to. It's as though we lived in a dark room. It's the playwright's job to illuminate and transform that room with all the means at his disposal, and finally to open the door—not to a dead end, but to yet another room.

—JOHN GUARE

The duty of dramatists is to express their times and guide the public through the perplexities of those times.

—ROBERT E. SHERWOOD

Immerse men in those universal and extreme situations which leave them only a couple of ways out, arrange things so that in choosing the way out they choose themselves, and you've won—the play is good.

—JEAN-PAUL SARTRE

A playwright must be his own audience. A novelist may lose his readers for a few pages; a playwright never dares lose his audience for a minute. In point of fact, I have to please myself, constantly.

—TERENCE RATTIGAN

When you've been hurt and you think you'll never have the courage to write another play, you must wait until a subject comes along that interests you enough to make you forget that you might be hurt again. It's like having a baby or falling in love. You must wait until something or someone comes into your life and calls you back. Then you say: I really love this material. I really want to tell this story. This time it doesn't matter whether or not they hurt me.

—MARSHA NORMAN

Some rules for writing a play:

    1. The story of a play must be the story of what happens within the mind or heart of a man or woman. It cannot deal pri-

marily with external events. The external events are only symbolic of what goes on within.

2. The story of a play must be a conflict, and specifically, a conflict between the forces of good and evil within a single person. The good and evil to be defined, of course, as the audience wants to see them.

3. The protagonist of a play must represent the forces of good and must win, or, if he has been evil, must yield to the forces of the good, and know himself defeated.

4. The protagonist of a play cannot be a perfect person. If he were, he could not improve, and he must come out at the end of the play a more admirable human being than he went in.

—MAXWELL ANDERSON

I used . . . to keep a book on which I would talk to myself. One of the aphorisms I wrote was, "The structure of a play is always the story of how the birds came home to roost."

—ARTHUR MILLER

I heard director Joshua Logan recount a conversation he'd had with Maxwell Anderson. . . . Was there one thing that had worked for [Anderson] above all else, one bit of advice he could give young playwrights? Anderson responded that the main character must learn something *about himself* before the end of the play, and that this must be something that would *change his life forever*. Only then would an audience feel satisfied enough to make the play a success. Logan asked why there must be such satisfaction, and Anderson said: ". . . because otherwise they walk out."

Such change is equally important in a short story or novel.

—PHYLLIS A. WHITNEY

(*See Dialogue, Screenwriting.*)

PLOT

On Tragedy

There are three forms of Plot to be avoided. (1) A good man must not be seen passing from happiness to misery, or (2) a bad man from misery to happiness. The first situation is not fear-inspiring or piteous, but simply odious to us. The second is the most untragic that can be; it has not one of the requisites of Tragedy; it does not appeal either to the human feeling in us, or to our pity, or to our fears. Nor, on the other hand, should (3) an extremely bad man be seen falling from happiness into misery. Such a story may arouse the human feeling in us, but it will not move us to either pity or fear. . . . The perfect Plot, accordingly, must have a single, and not (as some tell us) a double issue; the changes in the hero's fortunes must be not from misery to happiness, but on the contrary from happiness to misery; and the cause of it must lie not in any depravity, but in some great error on his part; the man himself being either such as we have described, or better, not worse, than that.

—ARISTOTLE

Plot depends for its movement on internal combustion.

—ELIZABETH BOWEN

I believe there are four main plots. They are as follows:

The Self vs. The Self	Internal Conflict
The Self vs. Another	Internal Conflict (Personal)
The Self vs. The State	External Conflict (Impersonal)
The Self vs. Time/Nature	Perspective Conflict

For 99 percent of all novels, conflict is the core of the plot. Without it there is no tension and there's no reason to turn the page. Essays are the place for gentle reflection. Novels are not.

The fundamental conflict of life is The Self versus The Self. *Hamlet* best exemplifies this story line.

—Rita Mae Brown

Questions to address in plotting:

What are the compulsions?
What are the obstacles?
Is the protagonist active? That is, does he make things happen, or is he one to whom things happen?
Is there a time crunch?

—Oakley Hall

We have defined a story as a narrative of events arranged in their time-sequence. A plot is also a narrative of events, the emphasis falling on causality. "The king died and then the queen died," is a story. "The king died, and then the queen died of grief," is a plot. The time-sequence is preserved, but the sense of causality over-shadows it. Or again: "The queen died, no one knew why, until it was discovered that it was through grief at the death of the king." This is a plot with a mystery in it, a form capable of high development. It suspends the time-sequence, it moves as far away from the story as its limitations will allow. Consider the death of the queen. If it is in a story we say "and then?" If it is in a plot we ask "why?" That is the fundamental difference between these two aspects of the novel.

—E. M. Forster

When the plot flags, bring in a man with a gun.

—Raymond Chandler

"Plot" isn't what compels many novelists to write, or some readers to read. But if you choose to write a novel without a plot, I would

178

hope three things for you: that your prose is gorgeous, that your insights into the human condition are inspirational, and that your book is short. I am directing my remarks, of course, to those writers (and readers) of *long* novels.

—JOHN IRVING

(*See Conflict, Emotion, Excitement, Form, Formulas, Scene/Setting, Story, Suspense.*)

POETRY

1st   I think poetry should surprise by a fine excess, and not by singularity; it should strike the reader as a wording of his own highest thoughts, and appear almost a remembrance.

2nd   Its touches of beauty should never be halfway, thereby making the reader breathless, instead of content. The rise, the progress, the setting of Imagery should, like the sun, come natural to him, shine over him, and set soberly, although in magnificence, leaving him in the luxury of twilight. But it is easier to think what poetry should be, than to write it. And this leads me to:

Another axiom—That if poetry comes not as naturally as the leaves to a tree, it had better not come at all.

—JOHN KEATS to John Taylor

That's the way I write a poem—getting a small piece of it in my hands and pulling it out and not knowing whether it is a man or a woman. I have never started a poem yet whose end I knew. Writing a poem is discovering.

—ROBERT FROST

All poetry is an ordered voice, one which tries to tell you about a vision in the unvisionary language of farm, city and love. Writing is like this—you dredge for the poem's meaning the way police dredge for a body. They think it is down there under the black water, they work the grappling hooks back and forth. But maybe it's up in the hills under the leaves or in a ditch somewhere. Maybe it's never found. But what you find, whatever you find, is always only part of the missing, and writing is the way the poet finds out what it is he found.

—PAUL ENGLE

Go to a big bookstore that has a lot of poetry books. Look them over and see if you find any affinity groups that you like among the little magazines and publishing groups, people you dig or who might dig your mind. Send them your stuff, just to connect with people you feel affinity with. Send your work to poets you like, and remember they get 20 books a week and can't read them all. They can only glance at them, and if they see something they like they will read it and respond.

—ALLEN GINSBERG

I never "draw lines." I make a rhyme conspicuous, to me at a glance, by underlining with red, blue, or other pencil—as many colours as I have rhymes to differentiate. However, if the phrases recur in too incoherent an architecture—as print—I notice that the words as a tune do not sound right. I may start a piece, find it obstructive, lack a way out, and not complete the thing for a year, or years, am thrifty. I salvage anything promising and set it down in a small notebook.

—MARIANNE MOORE

The business of the poet is to examine, not the individual, but the species, to remark general properties and large appearances; he does not number the streaks of the tulip. . . .

—SAMUEL JOHNSON

The modern poet may "number the streaks of the tulip" and not only think, but hope, that he has left it at that; but whether he likes it or not, he has said something new about flowers, and about men.

—MICHAEL HAMBURGER

The best poems are rich with observational truths. Above all, we ask the poet to teach us a way of seeing, lest one spend a lifetime on this planet without noticing how green light flares up as the setting sun rolls under. . . . The poet refuses to let things merge, lie low, succumb to visual habit. Instead she hoists things out of their routine, and lays them out on a white papery beach to be fumbled and explored. I don't mean to suggest that the subject of a poem is an end in itself. What it usually is, is an occasion, catalyst, or tripwire that permits the poet to reach into herself and haul up whatever nugget of the human condition distracts her at the moment, something that cannot be reached in any other way.

—DIANE ACKERMAN

A poet's mission is to make others confound fiction and reality in order to render them, for an hour, mysteriously happy.

—ISAK DINESEN

The best craftsmanship always leaves holes and gaps in the works of the poem so that something that is *not* in the poem can creep, crawl, flush, or thunder in.

—DYLAN THOMAS

Even when poetry has a meaning, as it usually has, it may be inadvisable to draw it out. . . . Perfect understanding will sometimes always extinguish pleasure.

—A. E. HOUSMAN

I wish our clever young poets would remember my homely definitions of prose and poetry; that is, prose—words in their best order; poetry—the best words in their best order.

—SAMUEL TAYLOR COLERIDGE

Cultivate simplicity, Coleridge, or rather, I should say, banish elaborateness; for simplicity springs spontaneous from the heart, and carries into daylight its own modest buds and genuine, sweet, and clear flowers of expression. I allow no hot-beds in the gardens of Parnassus.

—CHARLES LAMB to Samuel
Taylor Coleridge

True poets . . . wish neither to applaud nor revile their age; they wish to know what it is, what it can give them, and whether this is what they want. What they want, they know very well; they want to educate and cultivate what is best and noblest in themselves. . . . They do not talk of their mission, nor of interpreting their age, nor of the coming Poet; all this, they know, is mere delirium of vanity. . . . [The poet] will not, however, maintain a hostile attitude towards the false pretensions of his age; he will content himself with not being overwhelmed by them. He will esteem himself fortunate if he can succeed in banishing from his mind all feelings of contradiction, and irritation, and impatience.

—MATTHEW ARNOLD

It's very bad to use a rhyming dictionary, in my experience at any rate, because it means that the words you should think of at leisure, and mull over, and discover possibilities in, are given to you too suddenly, too easily, and you experience their possibilities superficially.

—RICHARD WILBUR

If you know what you are going to write when you're writing a poem, it's going to be average. Creating a poem is a continual process of re-creating your ignorance, in the sense of not knowing what's coming next. A lot of poets historically have described a kind of trance. It's not like a Vedic trance where your eyes cross, and you float. It's a process not of knowing, but of unknowing, of learning again. The next word or phrase that's written has to feel as if it's being written for the first time, that you are discovering the meaning of the word as you put it down. That's the ideal luck of writing a poem.

—DEREK WALCOTT

POINT OF VIEW

This involves the question of who tells the story. We may make four basic distinctions: (1) a character may tell his own story in the first person; (2) a character may tell, in the first person, a story which he has observed; (3) the author may tell what happens in the purely objective sense—deeds, words, gestures—without going into the minds of the characters and without giving his own comment; (4) the author may tell what happens with full liberty to go into the minds of characters and to give his own comment. These four types of narration may be called: (1) first-person, (2) first-person observer, (3) author-observer, and (4) omniscient author. Combinations of these methods are, of course, possible.

—CLEANTH BROOKS and ROBERT
PENN WARREN

A novelist can shift view-point if it comes off. . . . Indeed, this power to expand and contract perception (of which the shifting view-point is a symptom), this right to intermittent knowledge—I find one of the great advantages of the novel-form. . . . This inter-mittence lends in the long run variety and colour to the experiences we receive.

—E. M. FORSTER

183

I tried to tell it again, the same story through the eyes of another brother. That was still not it. I told it for the third time through the eyes of the third brother. That was still not it. I tried to gather the pieces together and fill in the gaps by making myself the spokesman. It was still not complete. . . . I never could tell it right, though I tried hard and would like to try again, though I'd probably fail again.

—WILLIAM FAULKNER

The first thing you gotta do is sit down and ask, Who's telling this story? Who grabs hold of you and says, Listen, I'm gonna tell you something that'll knock your socks off? He's a character. He speaks a particular way, sometimes uses profanity, sometimes he's a poet.

—LARRY FERGUSON

(See Omniscient Authors.)

POLITICAL WRITING

The political novelist must be able . . . to make ideas or ideologies come to life, to endow them with the capacity for stirring characters into passionate gestures and sacrifices. . . . No matter how much the writer intends to celebrate or discredit a political ideology, no matter how didactic or polemical his purpose may be, his novel cannot finally rest on the idea "in itself.". . . His task is always to show the relation between theory and experience, between the ideology that has been preconceived and the tangle of feelings and relationships he is trying to present. . . . For the writer the great test is, how much truth can he force through the sieve of his opinions? For the reader the great test is, how much of that truth can he accept though it jostle *his* opinions?

—IRVING HOWE

I mean to utter certain thoughts, whether all the artistic side of it goes to the dogs or not . . . even if it turns into a mere pamphlet, I shall say all that I have in my heart.

—FYODOR DOSTOYEVSKY

The political novel is a very various thing. . . . *The Charterhouse of Parma, Nostromo, Barnaby Rudge, A Tale of Two Cities,* and *All the King's Men* are all political novels, all very different in spirit. I think a successful political novel requires a knowledge . . . of the situation that once chooses to write about. Political commitment is not required, although eventually most authors maneuver themselves into a stand. I think the key is to establish the connection between political forces and individual lives. The questions to address are: How do social and political forces condition individual lives? How do the personal qualities of the players condition their political direction? . . . Because so much of serious politics in this century consists of violence, this can be a morally enervating exercise. Moral enervation is bad for writers.

—ROBERT STONE

The propagandist sees things as he thinks they should be. The novelist must see things as they are, because his purpose is to record and illuminate human experience. The goal of politics is to alter human nature, and often politics substitutes a system of delusion for reality. Joseph Brodsky, who has had some experience in politics, recently commented on this question: "Literature is a far more ancient and viable thing than any social formation or state," he said. "A writer should care about one thing—the language. To write well: that is his duty. That is his only duty. The rest is an attempt to subordinate the writer to some statesman's purpose." The novelist can't be a believer, because he must be a heartless observer.

—CHARLES MCCARRY

185

For me, writing fiction issues from the impulse to tell the story of people who deserve to have their lives examined and their stories told, to people who deserve to read good stories. I'm responsible to many people with buried lives: people who have been rendered as invisible in history as they are powerless in the society their work creates, populates, cleans, repairs and defends.

—MARGE PIERCY

When I want to write about political matters, I write essays or articles or give lectures. When I write literature, I concentrate on what is truly literature, something larger than politics. You can use politics for literature, but you cannot do the reverse.

—MARIO VARGAS LLOSA

(*See Message, Moral Position.*)

PRAISE

> Then teach me Heaven! to scorn the guilty bays,
> Drive from my breast that wretched lust of praise;
> Unblemish'd let me live, or die unknown:
> Oh! grant an honest fame, or grant me none!

—ALEXANDER POPE

Don't praise my book! Pascal had a nail-studded belt he used to lean against every time he felt pleasure at some word of praise. I should have a belt like that. I ask you, be a friend; either do not write to me about the book at all, or else write and tell me everything that is wrong with it. If it is true, as I feel, that my powers are weakening, then, I beg of you, tell me. Our profession is dreadful, writing corrupts the soul. Every author is surrounded by an aura

186

of adulation which he nurses so assiduously that he cannot begin to judge his own worth or see when it starts to decline.

—Leo Tolstoy to a friend

The rational pride of an author may be offended rather than flattered by vague indiscriminate praise; but he cannot, he should not, be indifferent to the fair testimonies of private and public esteem.

—Edward Gibbon

(*See Rewards.*)

PRECISION

Whatever the thing you wish to say, there is but one word to express it, but one word to give it movement, but one adjective to qualify it; you must seek until you find this noun, this verb, this adjective. . . . When you pass a grocer sitting in his doorway, a porter smoking a pipe, or a cab stand, show me that grocer and that porter . . . in such a way that I could never mistake them for any other grocer or porter, and by a single word give me to understand wherein the cab horse differs from fifty others before or behind it.

—Gustave Flaubert

This anxiety for external beauty which you reproach me with is for me *a method*. When I discover a bad assonance or a repetition in one of my phrases, I am sure that I am floundering in error; by dint of searching, I find the exact expression which was the only one and is, at the same time, the harmonious one. The word is never lacking when one possesses the idea.

—Gustave Flaubert to George Sand

Words in prose ought to express the intended meaning; if they attract attention to themselves, it is a fault; in the very best styles you read page after page without noticing the medium.

—SAMUEL TAYLOR COLERIDGE

The difference between the right word and the almost right word is the difference between lightning and the lightning bug.

—MARK TWAIN

When people say, "Gosh, it runs so smoothly," they don't realize that it's *hours* and *hours* and *hours* of honing each sentence, of removing one word, of lying in bed and thinking of *one* word that would be better in *one* place.

—JEFFREY ARCHER

For the effect you're trying to create, the precision in comedy writing is absolute. If you don't do it right, you don't trigger that laugh. To that extent it's good exercise.

—ANDY ROONEY

Just as with accuracy, there is precision of description as well as precision of fact. When you recount a concept, an idea, a program, a course of action—especially when it is someone else's—for the sake of your own credibility you have got to get the sense of it not only right, but precise. For example, this sentence is accurate but imprecise:

The mayor's program for reducing crime in the streets involves changes in the law itself and in the police department.

This is accurate and precise:

> The mayor's program for reducing crime in the streets involves stiffer prison terms for convicted criminals and a 50 percent increase in the number of police officers assigned to neighborhood patrol duty.
>
> —HERBERT E. MEYER and JILL M. MEYER

(*See Accuracy, Clarity, Details, Observation, Words.*)

PRIDE IN BEING A WRITER

Write to register history. . . . Write what should not be forgotten. . . . I feel that writing is an act of hope, a sort of communion with our fellow man. The writer of good will carries a lamp to illuminate the dark corners. Only that, nothing more—a tiny beam of light to show some hidden aspect of reality, to help decipher and understand it and thus to initiate, if possible, a change in the conscience of some readers. This kind of writer is not seduced by the mermaid's voice of celebrity or tempted by exclusive literary circles. He has both feet planted firmly on the ground and walks hand in hand with the people in the streets. He knows that the lamp is very small and the shadows are immense. This makes him humble.

—ISABEL ALLENDE

At best you affect the consciousness of your time, and so indirectly you affect the history of the time which succeeds you. . . . And the stakes are huge. Will we spoil the best secrets of life or will we help to free a new kind of man? It's intoxicating to think of that. There's something rich waiting if one of us is brave enough and good enough to get there.

—NORMAN MAILER

The nobility of our calling will always be rooted in two commitments difficult to observe: refusal to lie about what we know, and resistance to oppression.

—ALBERT CAMUS

I would like [my epitaph] to read, and it's going to take a lot of chiseling, it's going to take a big stone, but it should read: Here lies a teller of tales. If he had lived ten centuries ago, you would have walked down a street in old Baghdad or in some Middle Eastern city and there among the menders of copper and the shapers of clay turned into a Street of the Story Tellers and found him seated there among the tellers of tales who have existed since men came out of the caves. This is a proud heritage. This was his.

—RAY BRADBURY

This is a gift that I have, simple, simple; a foolish extravagant spirit, full of forms, figures, shapes, objects, ideas, apprehensions, motions, revolutions . . . But the gift is good in those in whom it is acute, and I am thankful for it.

—WILLIAM SHAKESPEARE, *Love's
Labor's Lost,* IV

(*See Aim, Ambition to Write, Joy in Writing, Perspective,
Purpose.*)

PRODUCTIVITY

If thou art a writer, write as if thy time were short, for it is indeed short at the longest. Improve each occasion when thy soul is reached. Drain the cup of inspiration to its last dregs. Fear no intemperance in that, for the years will come when otherwise thou wilt regret opportunities unimproved. The spring will not last for-ever. These fertile and expanding seasons of thy life, when the rain reaches thy root, when thy vigor shoots, when thy flower is bud-ding, shall be fewer and farther between. Again I say, remember thy Creator in the days of thy youth.

—HENRY DAVID THOREAU

I think there's a period in a writer's life when he is, well, simply for lack of any other word, fertile, and he just produces. Later on, his blood slows, his bones get a little more brittle, his muscles get a little stiff, he gets perhaps other interests, but I think there's one time in his life when he writes at the top of his talent plus his speed, too. Later the speed slows; the talent doesn't necessarily fade at the same time. But there's a time in his life, one matchless time, when they are matched completely. The speed, and the power and the talent, they're all there and then he is . . . "hot."

—WILLIAM FAULKNER

(See Doggedness, Effort, Persistence.)

PROFESSIONALISM

As for the amateur, his difficulty is that his work, once on the page, hardens as cement hardens and can no more be changed. When he has learned to change it, to consider it in this light, to consider it in that, to hold the subject warm in his affections at the same time that his mind appraises the form—when that time comes, he is no longer an amateur.

—EDITH RONALD MIRRIELEES

(See Artistry, Craftsmanship, Revision.)

PROTAGONIST

The pivotal character forces the conflict from beginning to end in a play, story, or novel. . . . If a writer doesn't understand the mechanism of a pivotal character, he won't know in what direction his story is going. . . . The pivotal character is the heart of all stories, pumping in all the conflict. If he stops pumping, your story or play stops living, just as your body would stop living if the bloodstream were cut off.

—LAJOS EGRI

There must be one central character. One. Everybody write that down. Just one. And he or she must want something. And by the end of the play he or she must either get it or not. Period. No exceptions.

—MARSHA NORMAN

It is the mark of a classic short story that there be but one major character, so complexity will be properly lavished there. Supporting characters had better be kept simple to prevent their stealing the story's focus.

—BARNABY CONRAD

(*See Characterization.*)

PUNCTUATION

All we can do is hang on to our colons: punctuation is bound to change, like the rest of language; punctuation is made for man, not man for punctuation; a good sentence should be intelligible without the help of punctuation in most cases; and, if you get in a muddle with your dots and dashes, you may need to simplify your thoughts, and shorten your sentence.

—PHILLIP HOWARD

The word "I'll" should not be divided so that the "I" is on one line and " 'll" on the next. The reader's attention, after the breaking up of "I'll," can never be successfully recaptured.

—JAMES THURBER

Every author has his own style and consequently his own grammatical rules. I put commas where I deem them necessary, and where I deem them unnecessary others must not put them! [And] remember that I never use superfluous commas: Never add or remove a single one!

—FYODOR DOSTOYEVSKY

PURPOSE

The business of the poet and novelist is to show the sorriness underlying the grandest things, and the grandeur underlying the sorriest things.

—THOMAS HARDY

Who am I and why was I born and what is it all for? Who are these others and what have they to do with me and what have I to do with them? To ask these questions is to seek the essentials of some sort of philosophy of life. And to answer them in one way or another is the meaning of literature. Whenever a book, through the direct voice of poetry or through the voices of characters in a novel, recognizes these fundamental questions of the human heart, that book is read and lives on and on. And whenever a book ignores them, though it achieves a momentary popularity, it passes on and is forgotten. Light upon the deep and primitive inquiry of the human heart is the primary contribution, then, of literature.

—PEARL S. BUCK

The aim of every artist is to arrest motion, which is life, by artificial means and hold it fixed so that a hundred years later, when a stranger looks at it, it moves again since it is life. Since man is mortal the only immortality possible for him is to leave something behind him that is immortal since it will always move. This is the artist's way of scribbling "Kilroy was here" on the wall of the final and irrevocable oblivion through which he must someday pass.

—WILLIAM FAULKNER

Is the story meant to entertain? To educate? To clarify? To experiment? To express beautiful words? To search for meaning? To demonstrate the importance of some concept? To show the value of humanity, or the lack of it? Is it meant to scare you? To please you? To excite you? To sadden you or make you happy? None of these requires exclusivity. Novels can include any combination of these and other purposes, and whether or not a book is popular has nothing to do with it. Commercial vs. literary is an artificial criterion for establishing the value of a book, based on economics, not merit.

—JEAN M. AUEL

The true artist plays mad with all his soul, labors at the very lip of the volcano, but remembers and clings to his purpose, which is as strong as the dream. He is not someone possessed, like Cassandra, but a passionate, easily tempted explorer who fully intends to get home again, like Odysseus.

—JOHN GARDNER

There is a profound human need to find a sense in life. . . . I am continuously trying to find the meaning of things under the text. It's against the cancer of exaggerated interpretation, in which you are never satisfied, you always want another answer.

—UMBERTO ECO

Writing is an affair of yearning for great voyages and hauling on frayed ropes.

—ISRAEL SHENKER

My life, like everyone's life, is a chaos, and the only continuous thread is literature. I have been a writer, and that's it. I have taken literature seriously above all else. The rest has been subordinated.

—ALBERTO MORAVIA

My purpose in writing is to connect all classes of people with one common bond of sympathy; to picture all grades of life in such a way that all grades will read, understand, and feel it, thus learning about each other and themselves . . . to touch and draw out that vein of poetry and feeling which exists somewhere in every human nature.

—WILL CARLETON

(See *Aim, Challenge, Dedication, Joy in Writing, New Writers, Pride in Being a Writer, Values.*)

195

PUTTING IT OFF

The Law of Delay: that writing which can be delayed, will be. Teachers and writers too often consider resistance to writing evil, when, in fact, it is necessary. . . . There must be time for the seed of the idea to be nurtured in the mind. Far better writers than I have felt the same way. Over his writing desk Franz Kafka had one word, "Wait." William Wordsworth talked of the writer's "wise passiveness." . . . Even the most productive writers are expert dawdlers. . . . Writers fear this delay, for they can name colleagues who have made a career of delay, whose great unwritten books will never be written, but, somehow, those writers must have the faith to sustain themselves through the necessity of delay.

—DONALD M. MURRAY

(*See Discipline, Doggedness, Momentum, Persistence.*)

Q

QUESTIONABLE ADVICE

Remember that you must never sell your soul. . . . Never accept payment in advance. All my life I have suffered from this. . . . Never give a work to the printer before it is finished. This is the worst thing you can do . . . it constitutes the murder of your own ideas.

—FYODOR DOSTOYEVSKY, advice
to a young writer

Literary success of any enduring kind is made by refusing to do what publishers want, by refusing to write what the public wants, by refusing to accept any popular standard, by refusing to write anything to order.

—LAFCADIO HEARN

If a writer has to rob his mother, he will not hesitate. The "Ode on a Grecian Urn" is worth any number of old ladies.

—WILLIAM FAULKNER

QUOTATION

[Emerson] says sharply, "I hate quotations. Tell me what you know." In his essay on quotations and originality he notes warmly, "Next to the originator of a good sentence is the quoter of it." You pays your money and you takes your choice (source unknown). . . . If you quote, do not be too nice in your quotation, or correct a man if he misquotes slightly. It is not pedantry to mention *fresh fields and pastures new.* It *is* pedantry to remind the speaker that Milton wrote *fresh woods.* Actually *fresh fields* is a slight improvement, at least for mnemonic purposes. Shakespeare wrote *An ill-favoured thing, sir, but mine own.* We generally say *A poor thing but my own,* and our slight updating of the phrasing rescues it for our time: a good thing, sir, and our own. To quote with aptness and with pleasure is more important than to quote with prissy correctness.

—CLIFTON FADIMAN

R

READING AS A WRITER

Be sure that you go to the author to get at *his* meaning, not to find yours.

—John Ruskin

Perhaps for a novelist it's detrimental to read too much. I've always had a fear of cluttering my mind with too much detail, when the point of the novel is to be able to make leaps into the imagination.

—William Styron

Writing is a difficult trade which must be learned slowly by reading great authors, by trying at the outset to imitate them; by daring then to be original and by destroying one's first productions.

—André Maurois

Consider a book in the light of what it can teach you about your own work. . . . Read with every faculty alert. Notice the rhythm of the book, and whether it is accelerated or slowed when the author wishes to be emphatic. Look for mannerisms and favorite words, and decide for yourself whether they are worth trying for practice or whether they are too plainly the author's own to reward you for learning their structure. How does he get the characters from one scene to another, or mark the passing of time? . . . How does he get contrast? Is it, for instance, by placing character against setting incongruously—as Mark Twain put his Connecticut Yankee down into the world of King Arthur's day?

—DOROTHEA BRANDE

Too many writers are trying to write with too shallow an education. Whether they go to college or not is immaterial. I've met many self-educated people who are much better read than I am. The point is that a good writer needs a sense of the history of literature to be successful as a writer, and you need to read some Dickens, some Dostoyevsky, some Melville, and other great classics—because they are part of our world consciousness, and the good writers tap into the world consciousness when they create.

—JAMES KISNER

Read as much as you can of the best writers, and read Shakespeare all through life. Compared to the rest of literature, he is like the Pacific Ocean compared to the chain of Great Lakes. The lakes are respectable, but they are NOT the Pacific Ocean. Read five or six books at a time.

Read books that tell you what your predecessors on the earth have believed and done, and how they escaped their superstitions. Read also some of the old classics. Plato's description of the men in a cave and of the trial and death of Socrates; more, if you can stand it. Read enough of Sophocles, Euripides, Aeschylus, to let you know how those powerful minds of antiquity expressed themselves.

Read a history of philosophy. . . . Read enough of Goethe, Schiller, Heine, Villon, Molière, Racine, Corneille, to know a little about the French and German mind. Read Dante and Cervantes. Not to know both is harmful ignorance. Read all you can of

200

Homer—enough to know just why Homer, Dante, Goethe, Cervantes and Shakespeare are the world's most famous writers.

In short, READ, always coming back to Shakespeare. And keep yourself to yourself, at least part of the time, remembering Goethe's true saying: *Es bildet ein Talent sich in der Stille, doch ein Karakter in dem Strohm der Welt.*" "Talent is built in the silence, character in the stream of the world."

—ARTHUR BRISBANE

A Multicultural Reading List

When the subject is minority or Third World cultures, the following "great books" should be required ... The *Bhagavad Gita* (Hindu) [one of a hundred books in the Upanishads] ... Confucius's *Analects* (Chinese) ... *The Koran* (Muslim) ... Lady Shikibu Murasaki's *Tale of Genji* (Japanese) ... Rabindranath Tagore's *Gitanjali* (Bengali) ... Chinua Achebe's *Things Fall Apart* (Africa) ... Naguib Mahfouz's *The Thief and the Dogs* (Egypt) ... Octavio Paz's *The Labyrinth of Solitude* (Mexico). ... Other classics that could be added to this list include the *Tao T' Ching of Lao-tse* ... and the *Rubaiyat* of Omar Khayyam. Contemporary works, such as Mario Vargas Llosa's *Against Wind and Tide,* V. S. Naipaul's *A House for Mr. Biswas,* the work of Jorge Luis Borges, and the novels of Wole Soyinka, could be used as well. Any multicultural curriculum should explore the principles of Buddhism.

—DINESH D'SOUZA

(*See Influences.*)

REALISM

You must show—not tell—that you know what you are talking about. That you've been there. That the subject's eyes are dark blue, her hair is the color of straw, her legs are lanky, and her movements are like those of a ballerina.

—LINTON WEEKS

Recording of everyday gestures, habits, manners, customs, styles of traveling, eating, keeping house, modes of behaving toward children, servants, superiors, inferiors, peers, plus the various looks, glances, poses, styles of walking and other symbolic details that might exist within a scene . . . is not mere embroidery in prose. It lies as close to the center of the power of realism as any other device in literature.

—TOM WOLFE

There is a narrow street between reality and imagination. We have begun to walk straight down that narrow street. The old realism didn't express the real. What I want to know is the essence, the really real, the inner as well as the outer reality.

—CESARE ZAVATTINI

(*See Fictional Realism vs. Neo-Fabulism, Imagination.*)

RECOGNITION

The good artist should expect no recognition of his toil and no admiration of his genius, because his toil can with difficulty be appraised and his genius cannot possibly mean anything to the illiterate who, even from the dreadful wisdom of their evoked dead, have, so far, culled nothing but inanities and platitudes.

—JOSEPH CONRAD

From the beginning, writers have been accused of justifying their art as the search for immortality. But no writer I know would feel for an instant that being remembered after one's death is adequate compensation for dying, much less an efficient motivation for the willful madness of artistic discipline. The immortality associated with writing lies in the writer's daily visit to an internal eternity.

—KENNETH ATCHITY

(See Fame, Praise, Rewards.)

REJECTION

First remember George Seither's rule: "We don't reject writers; we reject pieces of paper with typing on them." Then scream a little. . . . Don't stay mad and decide you are the victim of incompetence and stupidity. If you do, you'll learn nothing and you'll never become a writer. . . . Don't get huffy because you have already made sales and therefore feel that no editor dare reject you. That's just not so. He *can* reject you and he need not even offer any reason. . . . Don't make the opposite mistake and decide the story is worthless. Editors differ and so do tastes and so do magazines' needs. Try the story somewhere else. . . . What doesn't fit one magazine might easily fit another.

—ISAAC ASIMOV

[No one has determined who conceived the following "Rejection from a Chinese Editor," but he or she must have been an editor]:

Illustrious brother of the sun and moon—Behold thy servant prostrate before thy feet. I kow-tow to thee and beg of thy graciousness thou mayest grant that I may speak and live. Thy honored manuscript has deigned to cast the light of its august countenance upon me. With raptures I have perused it. By the bones of my ancestry, never have I encountered such wit, such pathos, such lofty thoughts. With fear and trembling I return the writing. Were I to publish the treasure you sent me, the Emperor would order that it should be made the standard, and that none be published except such as equalled it. Knowing literature as I do, and that it would be impossible in ten thousand years to equal what you have done, I send your writing back. Ten thousand times I crave your pardon. Behold my head is at your feet. Do what you will.

    Your servant's servant,

THE EDITOR

(*See Criticism, Discouragement.*)

RELEVANCE

Relevance crystallizes meaning. The novelist's—any writer's—object is, to whittle down his meaning to the exactest and finest possible. What, of course, is fatal is when he does not know what he does mean; he has no point to sharpen.

—ELIZABETH BOWEN

REMUNERATION

Write without pay until somebody offers pay. If nobody offers within three years the candidate may look upon his circumstances with the most implicit confidence as the sign that sawing wood is what he was intended for.

—MARK TWAIN

Literature is like any other trade; you will never sell anything unless you go to the right shop.

—GEORGE BERNARD SHAW to a
young author

Write out of love, write out of instinct, write out of reason. . . . But always for money.

—Louis Untermeyer

Dollars damn me; and the malicious Devil is forever grinning in upon me, holding the door ajar. . . . What I feel most moved to write, that is banned—it will not pay. Yet, altogether, write the *other* way I cannot. So the product is a final hash, and all my books are botches.

—Herman Melville

Never buy an editor or publisher a lunch or a drink until he has bought an article, story or book from you. This rule is absolute and may be broken only at your peril.

—John Creasey

Sir, no man but a blockhead ever wrote, except for money.

—Samuel Johnson

If you want to get rich from writing, write the sort of thing that's read by persons who move their lips when they're reading to themselves.

—Don Marquis

(*See Fame, Recognition, Rewards.*)

REPETITION

Have no unreasonable fear of repetition. . . . The story is told of a feature writer who was doing a piece on the United Fruit Company. He spoke of bananas once; he spoke of bananas twice; he spoke of bananas yet a third time, and now he was desperate. "The world's leading shippers of the elongated yellow fruit," he wrote. A fourth banana would have been better.

—JAMES J. KILPATRICK

REPORTING

How to Be a Better Reporter:

One: See a thing clearly and describe it simply.

Two: Keep in mind the great crowd that cannot afford to hire a corporation lawyer, but can afford a three-cent newspaper. Every newspaper man owes to his poorest reader the loyalty that a great lawyer owes to his richest client. Some newspaper owners forget that, especially after they become rich, and no longer remember how it feels to be poor.

Three: Write so that the reader will say, "I feel as though I had actually SEEN what the newspaper describes."

Four: In reporting, don't forget to bring back PICTURES. One good picture tells more than a thousand words, and this is the picture age.

Five: Write plain, simple English, avoiding "newspaper English." Don't be afraid to use the same word twice. Don't write "horse," then "equine," or "dog," then "canine," or "rat," then "rodent."

Avoid fancy writing. The most powerful words are simplest. "To be or not to be, that is the question," "In the beginning was the word," "We are such stuff as dreams are made on, and our little life is rounded with a sleep," "Out, out, brief candle," "The rest is silence." Nothing fancy in those quotations. A natural style is the only style.

Make your writing striking, and musical, if you can. Don't try for onomatopoeia. English, unlike German, Greek, and some other languages, does not lend itself to it. Never overdo "apt alliteration's artful aid."

Six: Feed your mind as you feed your body, EVERY day. Feed your body less, and your mind more, if you want to be a good newspaper man. A prizefighter can't fight on the beefsteak he ate ten years ago. Newspaper men can't do good work on the THINKING of twenty years ago. READ AND THINK. Keep your mind open to new ideas.

Write with difficulty. "Work, as nature works, in fire," was Dante's advice, quoted by D'Annunzio. If you do not burn as you work, readers will be cold as they read.

Seven: Learn to edit your copy. Strike out "very" always. Strike out most of your adjectives, remembering the wise Frenchman's remark: *"L'adjectif est l'ennemi du substantif."* "The adjective is the enemy of the noun."

—ARTHUR BRISBANE, Advice
posted in the office of J. Reagan
"Tex" McCrary

Checklist for writing a story:

Stick to the facts. Never *wish* facts.
When in doubt, attribute.*
Never insert your personal opinion.
Be discreet in the use of adjectives.
Avoid cheap shots.
Remember you are an observer, not a protagonist.
Listen to your editors—they will fire you if you don't.
Remember the children. Even thieves can have families. Try to put yourself in the place of the people you are writing about.

—LEONARD RAY TEEL and ROD
TAYLOR

*Attributes, such as "police said," "investigators charge," "witnesses responded," can clutter good writing but they can also save you from litigation. Never put yourself in the position of accuser, even if you can back up the allegations with documents and witnesses.

The writer must not invent. The legend on the license must read: None of This Was Made Up. The ethics of journalism, if we can be allowed such a boon, must be based on the simple truth that every journalist knows the difference between the distortion that comes from subtracting observed data and the distortion that comes from adding invented data.

—JOHN HERSEY

Let there be a fresh breeze of new honesty, new idealism, new integrity. And there, gentlemen, is where you come in. You have typewriters, presses, and a huge audience. How about raising hell?

—JENKIN LLOYD JONES

(See Journalism, Observation.)

RESOLUTION

The hardest thing to do is to write straight honest prose on human beings. First you have to know the subject; then you have to know how to write. Both take a lifetime to learn, and anybody is cheating who takes politics as a way out. All the outs are too easy, and the thing itself is too hard to do.

—ERNEST HEMINGWAY

(See Craftsmanship, Doggedness, Honesty, Integrity, Purpose.)

RESTRAINT

A Japanese emperor once asked a famous artist at his court to paint a four-panel screen of crows in flight. After much thought, the artist finally drew a single crow disappearing off the edge of the fourth panel of the screen. It was a masterpiece of movement. A great Oriental principle of drawing was fulfilled: "The idea must be present even where the brush has not passed."

—CHARLOTTE WILLARD

RETIREMENT

How should one adjust to age? In principle one shouldn't adjust. In fact, one does. (Or I do.) When my head starts knocking because of my attempt to write, I quit writing instead of carrying on as I used to do when I was young.

—E. B. WHITE

REVISION

If you write aught, read it through a second time, for no man can avoid slips. Let not any consideration of hurry prevent you from revising a short epistle. . . . A man's mistakes in writing bring him into disrepute; they are remembered against him all his days. As our sages say: "Who is it that uncovers his nakedness here and it is exposed everywhere? It is he who writes a document and makes mistakes therein."

—IBN TIBBON (c. 1190)

Read and revise, reread and revise, keep reading and revising until your text seems adequate to your thought.

—JACQUES BARZUN

Any fool can revise until nothing stands out as risky, everything feels safe—and dead. One way or another, all great writing achieves some kind of gusto. The trick lies in writing so that the gusto is in the work itself, and whatever fire the presentation may have comes from the harmony or indivisibility of presentation and the thing presented.

—JOHN GARDNER

You can teach yourself patience. If you can't bring yourself to put a finished manuscript away for a year to give yourself perspective when you look at it again, try six months. Four months. Three weeks. If you waste a day because you wrote nothing worth saying, don't worry about it. It comes with the territory. Don't hesitate to start a novel over, though you've been working on it for two years. Don't be afraid to change the protagonist or the ending, or to decide that you are not writing about the theme you originally had in mind. That's O.K.

—PHYLLIS REYNOLDS NAYLOR

I would imagine that most writers revise, one way or another. Maybe they don't revise as extensively on paper, but the process of writing is a process of inner expansion and reduction. It's like an accordion: You open it and then you bring it back, hoping that additional sound—a new clarity—may come out. It's all for clarity.

—JERZY KOSINSKI

"I rewrote the ending of A Farewell to Arms thirty-nine times before I was satisfied," Ernest Hemingway once told an interviewer. "Was there a problem there?" the interviewer wanted to know. "What was it that stumped you?"

"Getting the words right," said Hemingway.

—JUDITH APPELBAUM

Revise and revise and revise—the best thought will come after the printer has snatched away the copy.

—Michael Morahan

Interviewer: How many drafts of a story do you do?

Thirty-seven. I once tried doing thirty-three, but something was lacking, a certain—how shall I say?—*je ne sais quoi*. On another occasion, I tried forty-two versions, but the final effect was too lapidary—you know what I mean, Jack? What the hell are you trying to extort—my trade secrets?

—S. J. Perelman

(*See Cutting, Drafts, Editing, Marginal Notes, Outlining.*)

REVISION (EXCESSIVE)

Usually when I begin a new book, I am very pleased with it and work with great interest. But as the book work goes on, I become more and more bored, and often in rewriting it I omit things, substitute others, not because the new idea is better, but because I get tired of the old. Often I strike out what is vivid and replace it with something dull. . . . In a writer there must always be two people—the writer and the critic.

—Leo Tolstoy

(*See Cutting, Editing, Professionalism.*)

REWARDS

I should write for the mere yearning and fondness I have for the beautiful, even if my night's labors should be burnt every morning and no eye shine upon them.

—John Keats

But what is it to be a writer? Writing is a sweet, wonderful reward, but its price? During the night the answer was transparently clear to me: It is the reward for service to the devil. This descent to the dark powers ... of which one no longer knows anything above ground. ... And what is devilish in it seems to me quite clear. It is the vanity and the craving for enjoyment, which is forever whirring around oneself or even around someone else ... and enjoying it.

—FRANZ KAFKA

Writing is a way of coming to terms with the world and with oneself. The whole spirit of writing is to overcome narrowness and fear by giving order, measure, and significance to the flux of experience constantly dinning into our lives.

—R. V. CASSILL

Says the God of Art:
I shall give you hunger, and pain, and sleepless nights. Also beauty, and satisfactions known to few, and glimpses of the heavenly life. None of these you shall have continually, and of their coming and going you shall not be foretold.

—HOWARD LINDSAY

Nothing can so completely satisfy a life as to know it has something to do which it *can* do, and which at the same time is needed, and needed by the world at large. That would be my final message.

—WILLIAM ERNEST HOCKING

Q. What do you learn as a writer?
A. You learn things about yourself. You learn what you think.

The wonderful thing about writing is that you're constantly having to ask yourself questions. It makes you function morally. It makes you function intellectually. That's the great pleasure and great reward of writing.

—ROBERT STONE

The only reward to be expected for the cultivation of literature is contempt if one fails and hatred if one succeeds.

—VOLTAIRE

The most blessed thing about being an author is that you do it in private and *in your own time*. It can worry you, bother you, give you a headache; you can go nearly mad trying to arrange your plot the way it should go and you know it could go; *but*—you do not have to stand up and make a fool of yourself in public.

—AGATHA CHRISTIE

(*See Fame, Praise, Recognition, Remuneration.*)

RHYTHM

Effective writing . . . has to have cadence. By that, I do not mean metronomic regularity. I certainly don't mean that we should strive for a singsong effect; for if you get to be self-conscious, if you strive for rhythm only, you will wind up getting dizzy, you will sound like Hiawatha. And I pray you, sir, avoid it. No. I suggest only that we cultivate the inner ear. Let us listen to our sentences as they break upon the mind.

—JAMES J. KILPATRICK

The writer is not advised to try consciously for special rhythmic effects. He ought, however, to learn to recognize rhythmic defects in his own prose as symptoms of poor or defective arrangement of sentences and sentence elements.

—CLEANTH BROOKS and ROBERT
PENN WARREN

You don't write a sentence to get a certain rhythm. You write to say something.

—BILL STOUT

RULES

The first rule, indeed by itself virtually a sufficient condition for good style, is *to have something to say.*

—ARTHUR SCHOPENHAUER

It's not wise to violate the rules until you know how to observe them.

—T. S. ELIOT

Today you buy a bucket of paint and you're an artist, caress a microphone and you're a singer, gyrate your crotch and you're a dancer, take off your clothes and you're an actor, dump a ton of cement on the floor and you're a sculptor. Doing your own thing is all right for a genius. But, dear reader, you are not a genius. Neither am I. We need rules to build on. If you do something good *today,* it is bound to be modern.

—RUBE GOLDBERG

Any studied rules I could not possibly give, for I know of none that are of practical utility. A writer's style is according to his temperament, and my impression is that if he has anything to say which is of value, and words to say it with, the style will come of itself.

—THOMAS HARDY

(*See Content, Credos, Discipline, Form, Formulas, Structure, Style, Substance.*)

S

SATIRE

A man can't write successful satire except he be in a calm, judicial good-humor; whereas I *hate* travel, and I *hate* hotels, and I *hate* the opera, and I *hate* the *old masters*. In truth I don't ever seem to be in a good enough humor with anything to satirize it; no, I want to stand up before it and *curse* it, and foam at the mouth.

—MARK TWAIN

SCENE/SETTING

Nothing can happen nowhere. The *locale* of the happening always colours the happening, and often, to a degree, shapes it. Plot having pre-decided what is to happen, scene, scenes, must be so found, so chosen, as to give happening the desired force. Almost anything drawn from "real life"—house, town, room, park, landscape—will almost certainly be found to require some distortion for the purposes of plot. Remote memories, already distorted by the imagination, are most useful for the purposes of scene. Unfamiliar or once-seen places yield more than do familiar often-seen places.

—ELIZABETH BOWEN

My most productive associations as a writer have been, first and foremost, with places. I don't—I can't—put a thing in a place and start to work on it until I've been saturated in that place. And it takes years and years to arrive at that point. You have to know its civilization and its habits, and you have to like it.

—MARCIA DAVENPORT

(See Memory, Pace, Plot.)

SCIENCE FICTION

Professor J. B. S. Haldane once said, "The Universe is not only queerer than we imagine—it is queerer than we *can* imagine."

Nevertheless we must try. To write good science fiction, we must make the attempt somehow to reason and intuit our way to a vision that is at least somewhat as complex as reality.

—GARDNER DOZOIS

SCREENWRITING

Let me tell you the super story that Cliff Robertson told me a dozen years ago. . . . It was a story he had been told by Rosalind Russell. . . . She said, "Do you know what makes a good movie?" And he answered something like, "I don't know—good script, good actors, good cameramen and good directors, etc., etc." "No," she said. "Moments." She said, "A couple of moments that people remember, that they can take with them, is what makes a good movie."

—WILLIAM GOLDMAN

Your film must be *visual first, verbal second*. One of the most important techniques is the use of action to substitute for dialog. What characters do can, as in "real" life, speak louder about their motivations and intentions than what they say. The way two people run toward each other on a rainy street, stop, hesitate, then move forward and lock arms, can substitute for several lines of dialog. A safe rule to follow: Use action to speak for your characters as often as you can. Keep your motion picture in motion.

—CONSTANCE NASH and VIRGINIA
OAKEY

I understand one secret: The way you get screenplays on the screen is, you write parts that actors want to play. There are very few directors who can just sign on and make your movie, but I'm telling you, if you can get your script into Tom Cruise's hand and he says, "Oh, geez, I want to play this," guess what?

—LARRY FERGUSON

(See Dialogue, Playwriting.)

SECOND WIND

There is a moment when a heavenly light rises over the dim world you have been so long creating, and bathes it with life and beauty. Accept this omen that your work is good, and revel in the sunshine of composition.

—BENJAMIN DISRAELI

(See Boredom, Pace, Putting It Off.)

SECRECY

Writing is like sex. You have to save your love for the love object. If you go around spouting about your idea, when it comes time to go to bed with that idea, there'll be no "charge" left. You can't father children that way.

—RAY BRADBURY

I think it's bad to talk about one's present work, for it spoils something at the root of the creative act. It discharges the tension.

—NORMAN MAILER

The fewer writers you know the better, and if you're working on anything, don't tell them.

—MAEVE BRENNAN

I think it's a pretty good rule not to tell what a thing is about until it's finished. If you do you always seem to lose some of it. It never quite belongs to you so much again.

—F. SCOTT FITZGERALD

SELECTIVITY

If he is an artist, the realist will seek not to give us a banal photograph of life, but rather to give us the most complete, impressive, and convincing vision of life—more than reality itself is.

To relate everything would be impossible, because you would have to have at least a volume for each day in order to enumerate the mass of insignificant incidents that fill up our lives.

A choice therefore obtrudes itself—which is the first blow struck against a theory about "the whole truth." . . . The artist, having chosen his theme, only picks out details that are characteristic and of value for his subject, out of this life so burdened with chance and futility; and he rejects all the remainder and puts it to one side.

—GUY DE MAUPASSANT

I have learnt that I am *me,* that I can do the things that, as one might put it, *me* can do, but I cannot do the things that *me* would like to do.

—AGATHA CHRISTIE

Faulkner used to say, "Don't do what you can do—try what you can't do." Well, that can be overdone, too, because you can do something wild that you aren't equipped to do at all and fall flat. But I do think I am much in favor of being adventuresome.

—ELIZABETH SPENCER

SELF-REVELATION

Nothing goes by luck in composition. It allows of no tricks. The best you can write will be the best you are. Every sentence is the result of a long probation. The author's character is read from title-page to end. Of this he never corrects the proofs.

—HENRY DAVID THOREAU

If the stuff you're writing is not for yourself, it won't work . . . I feel I ought to write something because people want to read something. But I think, "Don't give them what they want—give them what you want."

—STEPHEN KING

I write to find out what I'm talking about.

—EDWARD ALBEE

There is no royal path to good writing, and such paths as do exist do not lead through neat critical gardens, various as they are, but through the jungles of self, the world, and of craft.

—JESSAMYN WEST

In one deep sense, novels are concealed autobiography. I don't mean that you are telling facts about yourself, but you are trying to find out what you really think or who you are.

—ROBERT PENN WARREN

(See Aim, Ambition to Write, Autobiography, Identity, Pride in Being a Writer, Purpose.)

SELF-STARTING

I have come up with a new simile to describe myself lately. It can be yours.

Every morning I jump out of bed and step on a landmine. The landmine is me.

After the explosion, I spend the rest of the day putting the pieces together.

Now, it's your turn. Jump!

—RAY BRADBURY

Every artist makes himself born. Your mother did not bring anything into the world to play piano. You must bring that into the world yourself.

—WILLA CATHER

(See Beginning, Effort, Inspiration, Motivation.)

SENTENCES

A sentence should read as if its author, had he held a plough instead of a pen, could have drawn a furrow deep and straight to the end.

—HENRY DAVID THOREAU

If your writing attracts your reader's attention, your style probably needs editing. Suspect all your favorite sentences. Each sentence must serve the whole.

—KENNETH ATCHITY

Sentences, which suggest far more than they say, which have an atmosphere about them, which do not merely report an old, but make a new impression, sentences which suggest as many things and are as durable as a Roman aqueduct: to frame these, that is the *art* of writing.

—HENRY DAVID THOREAU

[What to do when a sentence stinks]: Change it. How? Easy. Read a stinky sentence over. Figure out what it means. Now . . . put the sentence's meaning in your own words. . . . You may have to expand the sentence into two or three sentences. That's allowed.

—BILL SCOTT

" 'Tis the season to shower worldly goods on wordlovers." (*'Tis* is an itsy-pooism for *It is;* never use a construction that began in poetry and song and has been overworked by off-key holly-draped copywriters. Never start a sentence with *It is,* either; that sort of lollygagging up to a subject puts the reader to sleep.) That sentence should read, "Worldly goods should, in this season, be showered on wordlovers."

—WILLIAM SAFIRE

Take a piece of your prose and a red pencil and draw a slash after every sentence. Two or three pages ought to make a large enough sample. If the red marks occur at regular intervals, you have, as they used to say in the White House, a problem. Vary your sentence lengths. Naturally enough, complex patterns will fall into long sentences and emphatic conclusions work well when short. But no rules prevail except to avoid monotony.

—RICHARD A. LANHAM

(See Adjectives, Adverbs, Credos, Language, Verbs, Words.)

SENTIMENTALITY

That man has no soul . . . who can read of the death of Little Nell without laughing.

—OSCAR WILDE

I like grit, I like love and death, I'm tired of irony. As we know from the Russians, a lot of good fiction is sentimental. I had this argument in Hollywood; I said, "You guys out here in Glitzville don't realize that life is Dickensian." Everywhere you look people are deeply totemistic without knowing it: they have their lucky objects and secret feelings from childhood. The trouble in New York is, urban novelists don't want to give people the dimensions they deserve.

The novelist who refuses sentiment refuses the full spectrum of human behavior, and then he just dries up. Irony is always scratching your tired ass whatever way you look at it. I would rather give full vent to all human loves and disappointments, and take a chance on being corny, than die a smartass.

—JIM HARRISON

(*See Effect.*)

SEX

If the sex scene doesn't make you want to do it—whatever it is they're doing—it hasn't been written right.

—SLOAN WILSON

I write a lot of raunchy language. But then I write a lot of raunchy characters. You can't sit down and think, "Oh, my God, my maiden aunt is going to read this book." You have to be completely free when you write to do what you want to do, for your characters to do what they want to do.

—JACKIE COLLINS

I don't linger over sex scenes. . . . As for orgasms, I agree with the anonymous editor who advised: "There are two things that can't be described, and one of them is a sunset."

When Edith Wharton wrote *Ethan Frome* in 1911, she couldn't write a sex scene, so she had Ethan kiss Mattie's knitting wool instead. It's perfectly obvious what he's really doing, and the indirection of the writing makes it that much more powerful. The same is true of the single brief sex scene in *The French Lieutenant's Woman*. What makes it sexy is the buildup of tension between Charles and Sarah, the way the author made them strain toward each other like two dogs on a leash. The eroticism lies in the buildup.

—FLORENCE KING

I always start writing with a clean piece of paper and a dirty mind.

—PATRICK DENNIS

SHAPE

The shape of a great novel is whatever the author makes it, in as many words as he/she feels like. [Theodore] Dreiser never worried about word count. He'd get caught in a thought and carried away, loving the sound of music—his own.

I think of a fine old ballad ("These Foolish Things") where a guy finds in his ashtray a cigarette with lipstick traces, and falling into a soft-blue mood, flashes on other snippets and scraps from his last affair: two airline tickets, some painted swings, a tinkling piano. . . . The last verse gathers all the foolish things together to make the point of the song, not stated but implied: A good affair leaves sad-sweet memories, which will have to do him until his next love comes along. We're pleased because the end is just right for all that led to it, and rounds off the song, making a circle, which is the shape that satisfies.

—ROBERT TWOHY

I really begin with some kind of solid, coherent image, some notion of the shape of the book and even of its texture. *The Poorhouse Fair* was meant to have a sort of wide shape. *Rabbit, Run* was kind of zigzag, *The Centaur* was sort of a sandwich.

—JOHN UPDIKE

225

SHAPE OF IDEAS

Success in solving the problem depends on choosing the right aspect, on attacking the fortress from its accessible side.

—GEORGE POLYA

In your writing you must go over your material in your mind, trying to find the focus, the perspective, the angle of vision that will make you see clearly the shape of whatever it is you are writing about. There has to be one point that is sharply in focus, and a clear grouping of everything else around it. Once you see this clearly, your reader will see it too. And that, the shape of your ideas, is usually all he is going to carry away from his reading.

—RUDOLF FLESCH

Catch a friend who is interested in the subject and talk out what you have learned, at length. In this way you discover facts of interpretation that you might have missed, points of argument that had been unrealized, and the form most suitable for the story you have to tell.

—ALLAN NEVINS

(*See Effect, Focus.*)

SHORT STORY

In most good stories, it is the character's personality that creates the action of the story. In most of these stories, I feel that the writer has thought of some action and then scrounged up a character to perform it. You will usually be more successful if you start the other way around. If you start with a real personality, a real character, then something is bound to happen.

—FLANNERY O'CONNOR

In writing short stories—as in writing novels—take one thing at a time. (For some writers, this advice I'm giving may apply best to a first draft; for others, it may hinder the flow at first but be useful when time for revision comes.) Treat a short passage of description as a complete unit and make that one small unit as perfect as you can; then turn to the next unit—a passage of dialogue, say—and make that as perfect as you can. Move to larger units, the individual scenes that together make up the plot, and work each scene until it sparkles.

—JOHN GARDNER

Don't overwrite description in a story—you haven't got time. Don't bring in scenes that don't pertain to the central story. Don't bring in minor characters that might be nice in a novel to make a diversion, because again, you don't have time. But still try to keep the richness. Don't strip it down too far. I was never too partial to minimalist fiction for the reason it seems so stripped down that you hardly know where you are. So I think it's got to have some degree of fleshing out.

—ELIZABETH SPENCER

SILENCE

Whereof one cannot speak, thereon one must remain silent.

—LUDWIG WITTGENSTEIN

SIMILE

Keep your similes appropriate in style. A successful simile must fit its stylistic landscape as a hollow fits a circle. Robert Burns's beautiful "my luv is like a red, red rose" would be misplaced in a business article or a spy novel that requires less romantic imagery. . . . In Bernard Malamud's *The Natural* we have *a ball sailing through the light and up into the dark, like a white star seeking an old constellation;* in W. P. Kinsella's *Shoeless Joe,* the baseball field becomes a sensuous landscape—*cool as a mine, soft as moss, lying there like a cashmere blanket.* Such comparisons would be out of place if thrust into a newspaper's game story, but both are appropriate within the lyrical style of their novels.

—Elyse Sommer

(*See Figurative Expression, Metaphor.*)

SIMPLICITY

Simple English is no one's mother tongue. It has to be worked for.

—Jacques Barzun

SINCERITY

The only condition that I can think of attaching to the composition of the novel is . . . that it be sincere. This freedom is a splendid privilege, and the first lesson of the young novelist is to learn to be worthy of it. . . . Do not think too much about optimism and pessimism, try and catch the color of life itself.

—Henry James

One may write from the outside of the mind, as it were; write and write, learnedly and eloquently, and make no impression; but when he speaks from real insight and conviction of his own, men are always glad to hear him, whether they agree with him or not. Get down to your real self . . . and let that speak. One's real self is always vital and gives the impression of vitality.

—JOHN BURROUGHS

(*See Honesty, Integrity, Truth.*)

SLANG

Try and write straight English; never using slang except in dialogue and then only when unavoidable. Because all slang goes sour in a short time. I only use swear words, for example, that have lasted at least a thousand years, for fear of getting stuff that will be simply timely and then go sour.

—ERNEST HEMINGWAY

(*See Dialogue, Language.*)

SOLITUDE

Authentic art has no use for proclamations, it accomplishes its work in silence. To be altogether true to his spiritual life an artist must remain alone and not be prodigal of himself even to disciples.

—MARCEL PROUST

Between the crowd and ourself, no bond exists. Alas for the crowd; alas for us, especially. But since the fancy of one individual seems to me just as valid as the appetite of a million men, and can occupy an equal place in the world, we must (regardless of material things

229

and of mankind which disavows us) live for our vocation, climb up our ivory tower and there, like a *bayadère* with her perfumes, dwell alone with our dreams.

—GUSTAVE FLAUBERT

Writing is a solitary occupation. Family, friends and society are the natural enemies of a writer. He must be alone, uninterrupted and slightly savage if he is to sustain and complete an undertaking.

—LAURENCE CLARK POWELL

(*See Discipline, Environment.*)

SPEECHWRITING

"Let us" is particularly moving. It is most effective with women listeners, drawing them to the speaker. "Let us begin . . . Let us bind up the nation's wounds . . . Let us examine together . . . Let us never fear to negotiate." . . . *Leave the audience with something to remember.* What the speaker hopes to get across is a general impression of himself and one important point, one hammered-home phrase or slogan, one vivid image. An effective way to put across the point is to take the simplest approach: "The one thing I would like you to remember is this . . ."

Avoid euphemisms. Illinois Republican Everett Dirksen, the Senate Minority Leader, calls the euphemism "something that seems like what it ain't." On the Senate floor in 1964, he told a tale to explain the foolishness of euphemisms. "I am reminded of the man who filled in an application for an insurance policy. One of the questions he had to answer was 'How old was your father when he died and of what did he die?' Well, his father had been hanged, but

230

he did not like to put that in his application. He puzzled over it for quite a while. He finally wrote, 'My father was sixty-five when he died. He came to his end while participating in a public function when the platform gave way.' "

—WILLIAM SAFIRE and MARSHALL
LOEB

He [President Kennedy] disliked verbosity and pomposity in his own remarks as much as he disliked them in others'. He wanted both his message and his language to be plain and unpretentious. . . . He wanted his major policy statements to be positive, specific and definite, avoiding the use of "suggest," "perhaps" and "possible alternatives for consideration." . . . No speech was more than twenty to thirty minutes in duration. . . . His texts wasted no words and his delivery wasted no time. Frequently he moved from one solid fact or argument to another, without the usual repetition and elaboration. . . . He used little or no slang, dialect, legalistic terms, contractions, clichés, elaborate metaphors or ornate figures of speech. He refused to be folksy or to include any phrase or image he considered corny, tasteless or trite. He rarely used words he considered hackneyed: "humble," "dynamic," "glorious."

—THEODORE SORENSEN

I got my information on who the teacher was and what we should say from a researcher who got it from the advance office. I got my advice on the tone from Ben Eliott—don't go on too long, because it's hot in the Rose Garden and he's standing in the sun and reading from cards and that's not his best read. It's an annual speech— ask research for copies of what he's said in the past. "And remember, it always has to be positive with him. Never 'I'll never forget,' always 'I'll always remember.' "

I listened, I tried, I froze. The President would be saying these words! They were history! (They would go in the books!)

—PEGGY NOONAN

Never exaggerate. . . . Exaggeration is akin to lying and through it you jeopardize your reputation for good taste, which is much, and for good judgment, which is more.

—BALTASAR GRACIÁN

You must know your audience. If you're not already an insider, find out everything there is to know about the group, and tailor your remarks accordingly. If that's not worth doing, the speech isn't worth giving.

—ED WOHLMUTH

The ideal speech is about 20 minutes.

—ROBERT ORBEN

SPELLING

Bad spellers of the world, untie!

—GRAFFITO

SPIRITUAL QUESTS

Writing is my religion. . . . I do believe that somehow, no matter what the writing task, no matter how interesting or straightforward the technique, no matter how mercenary the reasons for writing it, if I search my soul and my heart I will find a way to capture some kind of energy, to somehow bring down a little fire to change my readers and change myself.

—DAVID BRADLEY

The problem that underlies everything I write [is] how to make man aware that he can build his greatness, without religion, on the nothingness that crushes him . . . we draw images from ourselves that are powerful enough to negate our nothingness.

—ANDRÉ MALRAUX

(See Purpose, Self-Revelation.)

STORY

Go and ask your grocer how he got started. You take something you've learned, something someone has said, and everything goes into the pot.

—PAUL GALLICO

Know the story—the whole story, if possible—before you fall in love with your first *sentence,* not to mention your first chapter. If you don't know the story before you begin the story, what kind of a storyteller are you? Just an ordinary kind, just a mediocre kind—making it up as you go along, like a common liar.

—JOHN IRVING

(See Beginning, Plot.)

STRUCTURE

Structure is everything. When authors come to me complaining of writer's block it means that they are too lazy to work out a structure either in their lives or in their work. Which is not to say that every writer doesn't have his own, idiosyncratic procedures. Mine begins with three basic stages: research, structure, and writing.

233

The writing part often takes the least time. I do all the reading and note taking for some months, or years if it's a long-term project with other books in between. Then I work on the structure for a long time. By the end it becomes a visual process, which I often do on the floor.

—Paul Johnson

The novel always starts with life, always has to start with life rather than an intellectual grid which you then impose on things. But at the same time, formally and structurally, I don't see why it shouldn't be inventive and playful and break what supposed rules there are.

—Julian Barnes

There are three rules for writing the novel. Unfortunately, no one knows what they are.

—Attributed to W. Somerset Maugham

The *structure* of the [novel] is usually balanced, efficient, economical, and tightly joined. A reader is left with the impression—which may be false in some cases—that the author has made a complete plan for the novel before setting to work on the first chapter. That is a comparatively safe method of writing novels and it has been followed by many distinguished authors. There are others, perhaps including more of the great, who have started with characters involved in a situation and allowed them to work out their own destinies. . . . Dickens and most of the famous Victorians began publishing their novels before they finished and before the novelists knew how the stories would end.

—Malcolm Cowley

Every novel should have a beginning, a muddle, and an end. The "muddle" is the heart of your tale.

—PETER DE VRIES

When you are stuck in a book; when you are well into writing it, and know what comes next, and yet cannot go on; when every morning for a week or a month you enter its room and turn your back on it; then the trouble is either of two things. Either the structure has forked, so the narrative, or the logic, has developed a hairline fracture that will shortly split it up the middle—or you are approaching a fatal mistake. What you had planned will not do. If you pursue your present course, the book will explode or collapse, and you do not know about it yet, quite. . . . What do you do? Acknowledge, first, that you cannot do nothing. Lay out the structure you already have, x-ray it for a hairline fracture, find it, and think about it for a week or a year; solve the insoluble problem.

—ANNIE DILLARD

(*See Form, Key Event, Outlining, Rules.*)

STYLE

Express yourself in a plain, easy manner, in well-chosen, signifi-cant, and decent terms, and give an harmonious and pleasing turn to your periods.

—CERVANTES

When some passion or effect is described in a natural style, we find within ourselves the truth of what we hear, without knowing it was there.

—PASCAL

If Tolstoy is so scornful of the music or words, it is because the only thing that matters to him is the thought behind them. His sentences, badly built, strung together with "who," "what," "which," "the latter," "the one who" and "as a result," express what he thinks all the better. After criticizing the old master's style, Chekhov wrote, "You read on and between the lines you see an eagle soaring in the sky, and the last thing in the world he cares about is the beauty of his feathers." True: Tolstoy's style is total freedom, absolute sincerity. He is the enemy of mystery in literature. His world is lighted full-face, brutally. Every shadow is defined by the position of the sun. No mirages, no phantoms, no sham. He bedevils his style for love of the truth as he bedevils his friends for love of the truth. If he could, he would live and write like a peasant: hammer words the way you hammer wooden wedges into a shoe sole. Make them stick, make it work, make it last for generations.

—HENRI TROYAT

There is nothing more dangerous to the formation of a prose style than the endeavour to make it poetic.

—J. MIDDLETON MURRY

Style is the saying in the best way *what you have to say*. The *what you have to say* depends on your age.

—MATTHEW ARNOLD

The first rule of style is to have something to say. The second rule of style is to control yourself when, by chance, you have two things to say; say first one, then the other, not both at the same time.

—GEORGE POLYA

I am glad you think my style plain. I never, in any one page or paragraph, aimed at making it anything else, or giving it any other merit—and I wish people would leave off talking about its beauty. If it has any, it is only pardonable at being unintentional. The greatest possible merit of style is, of course, to make the words absolutely disappear into the thought.

—NATHANIEL HAWTHORNE

These things [subject matter] are external to the man; style is the man himself.

—COMTE DE BUFFON

The whole secret of a living style and the difference between it and a dead style, lies in not having too much style—being in fact a little careless, or rather seeming to be here and there. . . . Otherwise your style is like a worn half-pence—all the fresh images rounded off by rubbing, and no crispness at all.

—THOMAS HARDY

Almost always prefer the concrete word to the abstraction. Almost always prefer the direct word to the circumlocution.

—ARTHUR QUILLER-COUCH

People think I can teach them style. What stuff it is. Have something to say and say it as clearly as you can. That is the only secret of style.

—MATTHEW ARNOLD

Style must always have an organic relation with the story. If you're telling a simple tale, then the style should be simple, but if you're dealing with very complex people, I don't think you can capture the quality of their minds without a style that is, syntactically speaking, complex.

—NORMAN MAILER

Place yourself in the background; write in a way that comes naturally; work from a suitable design; write with nouns and verbs; do not overwrite; do not overstate; avoid the use of qualifiers; do not affect a breezy style; use orthodox spelling; do not explain too much; avoid fancy words; do not take shortcuts at the cost of clarity; prefer the standard to the offbeat; make sure the reader knows who is speaking; do not use dialect; revise and rewrite.

—E. B. WHITE

Every book on writing you can find these days says essentially the same thing: Keep it short. Take it a bite at a time. Dispense with the adjectival frills. Put the punch in the verb and not the adverb (he added weakly). Edit, edit, edit, and avoid repetition. Less is more, spare is fair. Our taste in style matches our taste in corned beef: Lean is keen.

Maybe we are going overboard. The burst of the business memo, the snap-and-spit of the television news "bite," the mincing sentences of post-Hemingway novelists—all have led to the canonization of brevity. Introduce it, lay it out, sum it up. The dash is dead. It is not for nothing, as the Communists say, that the hottest word in communication is *briefing*.

—WILLIAM SAFIRE

By our handling of words we are often revealed or judged. "Has he written anything?" said Napoleon of a candidate for an appointment. "Let me see his *style*."

—F. L. LUCAS

The great struggle of a writer is to learn to write as he would talk.

—Attributed to LINCOLN STEFFENS

The writing style which is most natural for you is bound to echo the speech you heard when a child. English was the novelist Joseph Conrad's third language, and much that seems piquant in his use of English was no doubt colored by his first language, which was Polish. And lucky indeed is the writer who has grown up in Ireland, for the English spoken there is so amusing and musical. I myself grew up in Indianapolis, where common speech sounds like a handsaw cutting galvanized tin, and employs a vocabulary as unornamental as a monkey wrench.

I myself find that I trust my own writing most, and others seem to trust it most, too, when I sound most like a person from Indianapolis, which is what I am. What alternatives do I have? The one most vehemently recommended by teachers has no doubt been pressed on you, as well: to write like cultivated Englishmen of a century or more ago.

—KURT VONNEGUT

(See Dialogue, Flowery Style, Language, Slang, Technique, Tone, Voice, Words.)

SUBJECT

If you are going to write a novel the subject has to be very appealing: it really has to be something that draws you, even if it is painful, because you are going to have to live with it so long. I have no idea what my next subject is going to be, but I feel very free in doodling at the moment.

—IAN MCEWAN

I would hurl words into the darkness and wait for an echo. If an echo sounded, no matter how faintly, I would send other words to tell, to march, to fight.

—RICHARD WRIGHT

Find a subject you care about and which you in your heart feel others should care about. It is this genuine caring, and not your games with language, which will be the most compelling and seductive element in your style.

I am not urging you to write a novel, by the way—although I would not be sorry if you wrote one, provided you genuinely cared about something. A petition to the mayor about a pothole in front of your house or a love letter to the girl next door will do.

—KURT VONNEGUT

Ye who write, choose a subject suited to your abilities.

—HORACE

A writer should concern himself with whatever absorbs his fancy, stirs his heart, and unlimbers his typewriter.

—E. B. WHITE

And because I found I had nothing else to write about, I presented myself as a subject.

—MONTAIGNE

Before you undertake any piece of composition, you should try to frame the real subject, the central concern. You do not write about a house. You write about its appearance, the kind of life it suggests, its style or architecture, or your associations with it. You do not write about chemical research. You write about the methods of chemical research, the achievements of chemical research, or the opportunities for chemical research. You do not write about goodness. You write about the different kinds of goodness which have been held by different societies or religions at different times. . . . You must search your own thoughts and feelings to find your true subject.

—CLEANTH BROOKS and ROBERT
PENN WARREN

Oh, let me hurry and finish this book so I can start another. Now I see it clearly. If a book is to be any good, you have to love the central idea it expresses. In *Anna Karenina* I love the idea of the family, in *War and Peace* I loved the idea of the people, in my next book I shall love the idea of the Russian nation, as a rising force.

—LEO TOLSTOY

(*See Content, Motivation, Substance, Theme.*)

SUBSISTENCE

Look at the books of writers who have made it, whatever that means. You'll find that their first books were written like mine, at four o'clock in the morning while they had a full-time job. I wrote my first three that way, putting in a full day at the office, working in the early hours, but I was young then and had a lot of energy. I couldn't do it now, but that's what you have to do. Many writers can get jobs in public relations or elsewhere to supplement their incomes, and with the understanding of your spouse, you can organize your life so there is time to plug away at what you want to do. I believe in this thoroughly.

—JAMES MICHENER

I have learned that the heart of man, his body and his brain are forged in a white-hot furnace for the purpose of conflict. That

241

struggle for me is creation. Luxury is a wolf at the door and its fangs are the vanities and conceits germinated by success. When an artist learns this, he knows where the dangers lie. Without deprivation and struggle, there is no salvation and I am just a sword cutting daisies.

—TENNESSEE WILLIAMS

(See Creativity, Dedication, Discipline, Fame, Remuneration, Sustenance.)

SUBSTANCE

To write much, and to write rapidly, are empty boasts. The world desires to know *what* you have done, and not *how* you did it.

—GEORGE HENRY LEWES

[Writing is like splitting wood.] Aim past the wood, aim through the wood; aim for the chopping block.

—ANNIE DILLARD

It has always been much like writing a check. . . . It is easy to write a check if you have enough money in the bank, and writing comes more easily if you have something to say.

—SHOLEM ASCH

There is no surer way to make oneself a name than by writing about things which have a semblance of importance but which a reasonable man is not likely to take the time to investigate for himself.

—GEORG CHRISTOPH LICHTENBERG

(See Aim, Content, Message.)

SUBTLETY

Style, like the human body, is specially beautiful when the veins are not prominent and the bones cannot be counted.

—TACITUS

The most subtle, the strongest and deepest art—supreme art—is the one that does not at first allow itself to be recognized.

—ANDRÉ GIDE

Why talk in subtleties, when there are so many flagrant truths to be told? . . . [When an artist begins to say], "I am not understood, not because I am incomprehensible (that is, bad) but because my listeners-readers-spectators have not yet reached my intellectual level," he has abandoned the natural imperatives of art and signed his own death warrant by ignoring the mainspring of creation. . . . The artist of tomorrow will realize that it is more important and useful to compose a tale, a touching little song, a *divertissement* or sketch or light interlude, or draw a picture that will delight dozens of generations, that is, millions of children and adults, than a novel, symphony or painting that will enchant a few representatives of the wealthy classes and then be forgotten forever.

—LEO TOLSTOY

What I like in a good author is not what he says, but what he whispers.

—LOGAN PEARSALL SMITH

(*See Complexity, Obscurity, Suggestion.*)

SUCCESS

The work of a writer, his continuing work, depends for breath of life on a certain privacy of heart—and how is he to maintain it with that wreath on his head and that crowd at his heels?

—TENNESSEE WILLIAMS

Success is a continuing process. Failure is a stoppage. The man who keeps moving and working does not fail. . . . If you write a hundred short stories and they're all bad, that doesn't mean you've failed. You fail only if you stop writing. I've written about 2,000 short stories; I've only published about 300 and I feel I'm still learning. Any man who keeps working is not a failure. He may not be a great writer, but if he applies the old-fashioned virtues of hard, constant labor, he'll eventually make some kind of career for himself as a writer.

—RAY BRADBURY

Elements of a best-seller: (1) Write about a subject that you really know about. (2) Don't be hesitant about what you write. Don't worry about what people are going to think about you. Just write what you want to write. (3) Write it in your own particular style. (4) Write. Don't talk about it. Write it.

—JACKIE COLLINS

(*See Dedication, Discouragement, Fame, Rewards.*)

SUGGESTION

As a writer, you paint strokes and leave suggestions so readers can create their own pictures. That allows you to know someone by a small action and it saves countless pages of explanation.

—MARY HIGGINS CLARK

(*See Subtlety.*)

SURPRISE

Begin where the reader will be invited to do the most anticipating of the story, but where the reader will be the most compelled to guess wrong. If anticipation is a pleasure, so is surprise.

—JOHN IRVING

A story to me means a plot where there is some surprise . . . because that is how life is—full of surprises.

—ISAAC BASHEVIS SINGER

(*See Foreshadowing.*)

SUSPENSE

Always remember this: . . . the moment the hero announces what he thinks is going on, the cat's out of the bag.

—LARRY FERGUSON

In any work that is truly creative, I believe, the writer cannot be omniscient in advance about the effects that he proposes to produce. The suspense of a novel is not only in the reader, but in the novelist, who is intensely curious about what will happen to the hero.

—MARY MCCARTHY

(*See Focus, Plot.*)

SUSTENANCE

The thing I tell writers is: If you're going to take a job to live on, make sure it's a job that is impossible for you, just really unpleasant. That way, you won't ever get seduced into thinking, Gee, I really want to park cars all my life. That helps keep you on track. If you hate what you're doing every day, it reminds you of what you want to do.

—LAWRENCE KASDAN

The writer must earn money in order to be able to live and to write, but he must by no means live and write for the purpose of making money.

—KARL MARX

It gives a man character as a poet to have a daily contact with a job. I doubt whether I've lost a thing by leading an exceedingly regular and disciplined life.

—WALLACE STEVENS

I urge young writers not to be too much concerned with the vagaries of the marketplace. Not everyone can make a first-rate living as a writer, but a writer who is serious and responsible about his work, and life, will probably find a way to earn a decent living, if he or she writes well. A good writer will be strengthened by his good writing at a time, let us say, of the resurgence of ignorance in our culture. I think I have been saying that a writer must never compromise with what is best in him in a world defined as free.

—BERNARD MALAMUD

(See Career Path, Remuneration, Rewards, Subsistence.)

SYMPATHY

No novel is anything, for the purposes either of comedy or tragedy, unless the reader can sympathize with the characters whose names he finds upon the pages. Let an author so tell his tale as to touch his reader's heart and draw his tears, and he has, so far, done his work well. Truth let there be—truth of description, truth of character, human truth as to men and women. If there be such truth, I do not know that a novel can be too sensational.

—ANTHONY TROLLOPE

Learn to make yourself akin to people. . . . But let this sympathy be not with the mind—for it is easy with the mind—but with the heart, with love towards them.

—Russian writer (probably
Chekhov), quoted by Virginia
Woolf

(See Characterization, Compassion.)

SYNONYMY

Whatever you want to say, there is only one way to express it, one verb to set it in motion and only one adjective to describe it.

—GUY DE MAUPASSANT

(See Clarity, Words.)

T

TALENT/GENIUS

Talent alone cannot make a writer. There must be a man behind the book.

—Ralph Waldo Emerson

Do you know how to make your way in this world? By brilliant genius or by skilful corruption. You must cut your way through the masses like a cannon ball, or steal through them like a pestilence. Men bow before the power of genius; they hate it and try to slander it, because genius does not divide the spoil; but if genius persists, they bow before it. To sum it all up in a phrase, if they fail to smother genius in the mud, they fall on their knees and worship it. Corruption is a great power in the world, and talent is scarce. So corruption is the weapon of superfluous mediocrity.

—Honoré de Balzac

TECHNIQUE

Let the writer take up surgery or bricklaying if he is interested in technique. There is no mechanical way to get the writing done, no shortcut. The young writer would be a fool to follow a theory. Teach yourself by your own mistakes; people learn only by error. The good artist believes that nobody is good enough to give him advice. He has supreme vanity. No matter how much he admires the old writer, he wants to beat him.

—WILLIAM FAULKNER

A good rule for writers; do not explain overmuch.

—W. SOMERSET MAUGHAM

Every novelist ought to invent his own technique, that is the fact of the matter. Every novel worthy of the name is like another planet, whether large or small, which has its own laws just as it has its own flora and fauna.

—FRANÇOIS MAURIAC

(See Creativity, Style, Voice.)

TELEVISION WRITING

The big job is to create images; those just suggested in stories are not usually right for television. What you trust your reader to imagine just doesn't work.

—WILLIAM TREVOR

The writer's state of mind is important, too. If he rarely sees a televised show and thinks of his television set as a "boob tube," he will waste his time and talent trying to write for it. He must remember that he is writing not for the public but for the producers who believe, honestly enough, that they know what the public wants.

—Isabelle Ziegler

(*See Dialogue, Screenwriting.*)

TENSION

Remember that tension created for its own sake is cheap; no one will read your story more than once. The tension is part of your technique but technique is only a means to an end; it is never the end itself. That is why the French "new novel" is so boring—it has no capacity to move us—while older, stormy works like *Wuthering Heights* (which could only be "camp" to today's *avant-garde*) will be interesting to all imaginable future generations. I think the stress placed today on technique is misleading. A writer should imagine his scenes dramatically, as if they were to take place on the stage. There, empty, wordy passages are found out at once.

—Joyce Carol Oates

(*See Emotion, Plot, Suspense, Technique.*)

THEME

One often hears of writers that rise and swell with their subject, though it may seem but an ordinary one. How, then, with me, writing of this Leviathan? Unconsciously my chirography expands into placard capitals. Give me a condor's quill! Give me Vesuvius' crater for an inkstand . . . so magnifying is the virtue of a large and liberal theme! We expand to its bulk. To produce a mighty book, you must choose a mighty theme. No great and enduring volume can ever be written on the flea, though many there be who have tried it.

—Herman Melville

They say great themes make great novels . . . but what these young writers don't understand is that there is no greater theme than men and women.

—John O'Hara

If you sometimes confuse plot with theme, keep the two elements separate by thinking of theme as what the story is about, and plot as the situation that brings it into focus. You might think of theme as the message of the story—the lesson to be learned, the question that is asked, or what it is the author is trying to tell us about life and the human condition. Plot is the action by which this truth will be demonstrated.

—Phyllis Reynolds Naylor

This idea, or theme, is not necessarily a moral, such as "crime does not pay," or a message, "fortune favors the brave," although it may be; the story idea is an observation. If it poses a problem, that problem need not be solved, only observed. The theme may be specifically stated by the author, as in Katherine Anne Porter's "The Circus," or left to be inferred by the reader. But the theme is there all the time, illuminating and giving significance to all the details. If the story is well-written, the reader will find himself absorbed by the action, engrossed by the characters; but by the time he lays the story down, he should be aware of the author's vision of the world.

—Ralph H. Singleton and
Stanton Millet

The basic rule you gave us was simple and heartbreaking. A story to be effective had to convey something from writer to reader, and the power of its offering was the measure of its excellence. Outside of that, you said, there were no rules. A story could be about anything and could use any means and any technique at all—so long as it was effective. As a subhead to this rule, you maintained that it seemed to be necessary for the writer to know what he wanted to say, in short, what he was talking about. As an exercise we were to try reducing the meat of a story to one sentence, for only then could we know it well enough to enlarge it to three or six or ten thousand words.

—JOHN STEINBECK, in preface to
Story Writing, by Edith Ronald
Mirrielees, his story writing
teacher at Stanford University

The premise is the seed from which the story grows. The premise is the thumbnail synopsis of the story or play you wish to write. It isn't compulsory, but it is wise to formulate your premise first. You might have an idea or have read or heard something that seems to constitute a good story idea. No matter where your inspiration comes from, you must know exactly what you want to say, why you want to say it, and how far you want to carry it.

If your story pertains to greed, to which you are opposed, you'll want to know in what direction and how far you intend to go with this idea, what will be its final resolution. This crystallization of your story is your premise.

—LAJOS EGRI

(*See Good vs. Evil, Message, Moral Position, Nonfiction: Themes, Purpose.*)

TIME

Unless the writer is trying to exhibit confusion, the time of a happening in the story and the intervals between happening and happening must be kept clear in the reader's mind. Every happening has not only a time of its own but also a time relation to other

happenings. What these relations are, it is essential to show. . . .
Witness John Russell in *The Fourth Man:*

> But at sunrise, as if some spell had been raised by the clang of
> that great copper gong in the east . . . Under the heat of the
> day . . . By the middle of the afternoon . . . When the wind
> fell at sunset . . . Through that long clear night of stars . . . It
> was an evil dawning.

The very simplicity of the wording renders it inconspicuous, and
the reader is never at a loss for the progress of the tragic drama he
watches.

—Edith Ronald Mirrielees

TIME BOMBS

A "time bomb" in a novel is the presentation of a complication
facing the protagonist which must be resolved within a certain
period of time. . . . In some novels the "time bomb" is the major
complication, and the entire novel depends on it to hold interest.
A classic example is *Robinson Crusoe* by Defoe. Can Robinson
Crusoe survive on the island without dying or going insane before
he is rescued? *The Spy Who Came In from the Cold* employs this
principle. Can Leamas succeed in carrying out his mission for
Control before his masquerade as a defector is discovered by East
German Intelligence?

—Robert C. Meredith and John
Fitzgerald

TITLES

It is important to know the title before you begin—then you know
what you are writing about.

—Nadine Gordimer

A young first-time novelist hesitantly approached Somerset Maugham for aid in coming up with a title for his opus.

"Any drums in the book?" asked Maugham. No.

"Any trumpets?" Uh-uh.

"Then call it 'No Drums, No Trumpets.' "

Coming up with the right title—the magic combination of words that will turn browsers into buyers—is crucial to the success of a book.

—Joanne Kaufman

TONE

Every piece of writing has a tone: serious, flippant, formal, informal, aggressive, friendly, forceful, gentle, nasty, cheerful, and so forth. You can choose whatever tone you want—whichever one you find most appropriate, most comfortable, and which you believe will achieve the goals of your particular piece of writing. But once you make the choice, you must stick with it all the way through.

—Herbert E. Meyer and Jill M. Meyer

Tone has three main strands: the writer's attitude toward subject, reader, and self. . . . Writers may be angry about a subject or amused by it or discuss it dispassionately. They may treat readers as intellectual inferiors . . . or as friends with whom they are talking. . . . It behooves you, then, to create an appropriate tone and to avoid those—pomposity, say, or flippancy—which will put readers off. . . . In exposition it is often a good tactic to present yourself deferentially. . . . An occasional "it seems to me" or "I think" or "to my mind" goes a long way toward avoiding a tone of cocksureness and restoring at least a semblance of two-way traffic on that unavoidably one-way street from writer to reader.

—Thomas S. Kane

The tone of a writer's narrating voice is revealed in the writer's attitude toward his raw material or his subject. . . . The author's distance in relation to his story affects the tone. By becoming too chummy with the reader, the writer commits the cute-tone fallacy, characteristic at one end of the literary spectrum of many women's magazine stories and at the other end "little" or underground magazine fiction.

—DAVID MADDEN

(*See Attitude, Essay, Mood.*)

TRUTH

What you must study is mankind in general, and your own heart, and the truly great writers. As for me, I am only the exponent of a period of transition, meaningful only for individuals who are themselves in a state of transition.

Would to God your horizon may broaden every day! The people who bind themselves to systems are those who are unable to encompass the whole truth and try to catch it by the tail; a system is like the tail of truth, but truth is like a lizard: it leaves its tail in your fingers and runs away, knowing full well that it will grow a new one in a twinkling.

—IVAN TURGENEV, letter to
Tolstoy

Do not consider it proof just because it is written in books, for a liar who will deceive with his tongue will not hesitate to do the same with his pen.

—MAIMONIDES

Jean Malaquais once said, . . . "The only time I know that something is true is at the moment I discover it in the act of writing." I think it's that. I think it's this moment when one knows it's true. One may not have written it well enough for others to know, but you're in love with the truth when you discover it at the point of a pencil. That, in and by itself, is one of the few rare pleasures of life.

—NORMAN MAILER

A writer's problem does not change. He himself changes, but his problem remains the same. It is always how to write truly and, having found what is true, to project it in such a way that it becomes a part of the experience of the person who reads it.

—ERNEST HEMINGWAY

The value of every story depends on its being true. A story is a picture either of an individual or of human nature in general; if it be false, it is a picture of nothing.

—SAMUEL JOHNSON

(*See Honesty, Integrity, Sincerity.*)

u

UNCONSCIOUS

When the conscious mind is . . . stalled, the unconscious incubation stage begins. The poet Amy Lowell spoke of dropping the subject of a poem into her mind "much as one drops a letter into a mailbox," and Norman Mailer said that "In writing you have to be married to your unconscious. You choose a time and say, 'I'll meet you there tomorrow,' and your unconscious prepares something for you."

—OAKLEY HALL

UNDERSTATEMENT

Writing emotionally is risky. *Trying* to evoke emotions in your writing is deadly. Perhaps the best way to write emotionally is to not write emotionally at all, but to find something extraordinarily emotional and write about it with understatement. As a device, understatement can be used to drive home tragedy, poignance, sadness, terror and humor.

—LINTON WEEKS

(*See Emotion.*)

UPLIFT

It has never struck me as harmful to make a conscious effort to elevate one's thoughts, in the hope that by doing so one's writing will get off the ground, even if only for a few seconds (like Orville Wright) and to a low altitude.

—E. B. WHITE

URGENCY

It's important that a novel be approached with some urgency. Spend too long on it, or have great gaps between writing sessions, and the unity of the work tends to be lost.

—ANTHONY BURGESS

Never get sick, Hubert, there isn't time.

—HUBERT HUMPHREY's father

(*See Approaches.*)

V

VALUES

The artist never forces anyone to anything. He merely makes his case the strongest case possible. He lights up the darkness with a lightning flash, protects his friends the gods—that is, values—and all humanity, without exception, and then moves on. . . . I agree with Tolstoy that the highest purpose of art is to make people good by choice.

—John Gardner

(*See Aim, Good vs. Evil, Moral Position, Purpose.*)

VARIANTS

I've collected a host of "needless variants" (Fowler's term) over the years. . . . My favorite is "coronate" (for crown), a word which appeared in the *Times Magazine* itself a few years ago.

—Arthur L. Block

When a fielder doesn't chase a fly hard enough, Phil Rizzuto likes to say that he "nonchalanted" the ball.

—Stephen B. Labunski

(*See Language.*)

259

VERBS

Don't Depend on Adjectives, Use Strong Verbs: . . . In the sentence: "The woman sat thinking about how to get revenge on her husband," "thinking" is the verb. In this case it is not a strong verb. What the sentence needs is not a bigger word than "thinking" but rather one that is not associated with revenge. For example, "The woman sat embroidering revenge." . . . [But] don't reach too far for a verb and come up with . . . Purple Prose. . . . Describing a person as "a fellow toiler in the factory of life" is indeed purple prose.

—JUDY DELTON

(See Adjectives, Adverbs, Language, Sentences, Words.)

VISION

If there is one gift more essential to the novelist than another it is the power of combination—the single vision. The success of the masterpieces seems to lie not so much in their freedom from faults—indeed we tolerate the grossest errors in them all—but in the immense persuasiveness of a mind which has completely mastered its perspective.

—VIRGINIA WOOLF

(See Focus, Perspective, Theme.)

VOICE

[Writing in the third person] will probably work best for your first novels because it assists you in seeing your characters objectively, as fictional mechanisms rather than as extensions of yourself.

—KENNETH ATCHITY

Resolve not to use the passive voice. Simply fly in the face of convention and begin your sentences with "I" or "we" or "the writer."

—SHERIDAN BAKER

[Responding to interviewer's comment: "Your early plays seem to have a certain 'style,' which is a different thing from a 'voice.' "]

It is. Style is the outer trappings, and *voice* is even different from language, which is a manifestation of something. But a "voice" is almost without words . . . it's something in the spaces, in between.

—SAM SHEPARD

I try not to let my voice be the dominant one. It's hard to do that. The limitation of the great stylists—Henry James, say, or Hemingway—is that you remember their voices long after you've forgotten the voices of any of the people they wrote about. In one of the Psalms, God says, "Be still and know that I am God." I've always taken that to be good literary advice, too. Be still the way Tolstoy is still, be still the way Anthony Trollope is still, so that your characters can become gods and speak for themselves and come alive in their own way.

—FREDERICK BUECHNER

Experienced writers rarely begin a first draft until they hear in their heads—or on the page—a voice that may be right. . . . Voice carries the writer's intensity and glues together the information that the reader needs to know. . . . We speak differently at a funeral or a party, in church or in the locker room, at home or with strangers. We are experienced in using our individual voices for many purposes. We have to learn to do the same thing and to hear a voice in our head that may be polished and developed on the page. . . . Keep reading aloud as you draft and edit.

—Donald M. Murray

Dr. Don's Rule for Distinguished Writing:

It's in the voice. You get a call from a friend, you know right away who it is. One paragraph, you know the voice.

—Donald Newlove

(*See Mood, Style, Technique, Tone.*)

W

WITNESS

The artist ought not to judge his characters or what they say, but be only an unbiased witness . . . it is the jurors, that is, the readers, who will evaluate it. My business is to be talented, that is, to be able to distinguish important testimony from trivia, to illuminate the figures and speak their language.

—ANTON CHEKHOV

I think the ultimate responsibility of the writer . . . is to the idea of witness: This is what I see, this is what I feel, this is the way I think things are. Writers have the responsibility not to corrupt that point of view and not to be fearful of it, not to self-censor it. There's a certain dogged and sometimes foolish connection to the ideal of just telling the truth—seeing into the delusions, the self-deceptions, the lies, the pipe dreams, including his own.

—E. L. DOCTOROW

(See Objectivity.)

WOMEN WRITERS

I don't really feel limitations in writing as a woman. I feel I can see the point of view of a man. Once you've leaped into looking at the point of view of another person, I don't think it matters whether it's a man or a woman.

—EUDORA WELTY

I'm a playwright. But I'm a woman first. I am not a generic play-wright. I am a woman playwright. And I would hope that my choice of words and my choice of characters and situations reflect my experience as a woman on the planet. I don't have anything that I can add to the masculine perception of the world. What I can add has to be from what I've experienced. And my perceptions and my syntax, my colloquialisms, my preoccupations, are founded in race and gender.

—NTOZAKE SHANGE

A writer is a writer. You care about writing. It isn't men or women. I find these feminists very annoying, putting together these anthol-ogies of women writers. As if there were a difference. You sit down, you write, you are not a woman, or an Italian. You are a writer.

—NATALIA GINZBURG

WORDS

Prefer the familiar word to the far-fetched.
Prefer the concrete to the abstract.
Prefer the single word to the circumlocution.
Prefer the short word to the long.

Prefer the Saxon word to the Romance.

—H. W. and F. G. FOWLER

Short words are best and the old words when short are best of all.

—WINSTON S. CHURCHILL

The price of learning to use words is the development of an acute self-consciousness. Nor is it enough to pay attention to words only when you face the task of writing—that is like playing the violin only on the night of the concert. You must attend to words when you read, when you speak, when others speak. Words must become ever present in your waking life, an incessant concern, like color and design if the graphic arts matter to you, or pitch and rhythm if it is music, or speed and form if it is athletics.

—JACQUES BARZUN

Think of a word as a pendulum instead of a fixed entity. A word can sweep by your ear and by its very sound suggest hidden meanings, preconscious association. Listen to these words: blood, tranquil, democracy. You know what they mean literally but you have associations with those words that are cultural, as well as your own personal associations.

—RITA MAE BROWN

The best way to offset the harm of vogues is to stick resolutely, in speech and writing, to each vogue word's central meaning. *Address* an audience or a postcard, but not a problem or a question. Call a substance or a temperament *volatile,* but not an issue or a situation. Express sympathy far and wide, but keep *empathy* for aesthetics or psychiatry. Remember *Tiny* Tim and avoid naming things *minuscule* or *minimal*.

—JACQUES BARZUN

One of your first jobs, as you write for money, will be to get rid of your vocabulary.

—JACK WOODFORD

It is a frequently given piece of advice, 'not to use a long word where a short one would do,' but it may be acted upon too much. I would rather advise young writers to choose the word which best expresses their meaning, be it long or short.

—LOUISE MOLESWORTH

The written word
Should be clean as bone
Clear as light
Firm as stone.
Two words are not
As good as one.

—ANON.

Words have to be crafted, not sprayed. They need to be fitted together with infinite care. William Faulkner would isolate himself in a small cell-like room and labor over his words like a jeweler arranging tiny jewels in a watch. Thomas Mann would consider himself lucky if, after a full day at his desk, he was able to put down on paper 500 words that he was willing to share with the world.

—NORMAN COUSINS

We need words that will make us laugh, wonder, work, think, aspire, and hope. We need words that will leap and sing in our souls. We need words that will cause us to face up to life with a fighting faith and contend for those ideals that have made this the greatest nation on earth.

—Dr. E. C. Nance

(*See Credos, Dialogue, Grammar, Language, Slang, Style.*)

WORK PROCESS

Virginia Woolf was a slow writer . . . Yet she was comparatively a prolific writer. She wrote nine full-length novels, two biographies, and there are seven volumes of literary criticism; in addition to this there must be at least 500,000 words of her unpublished diaries. . . . Every morning, at about 9:30 after breakfast, each of us, as if moved by a law of unquestioned nature, went off and "worked" until lunch at one. It is surprising how much one can produce in a year, whether of buns or books or pots or pictures, if one works hard and professionally for three and a half hours every day for 550 days. That was why, despite her disabilities, Virginia was able to produce so much.

—Leonard Woolf

I would write a book, or a short story, at least three times—once to understand it, the second time to improve the prose, and a third to compel it to say what it still must say. Somewhere I put it this way: first drafts are for learning what one's fiction wants him to say. Revision is one of the exquisite pleasures of writing: "The men and things of today are wont to lie fairer and truer in tomorrow's meadow," Henry Thoreau said.

—Bernard Malamud

WORK STATION

Never forget that you own the telephone, the telephone does not own you. Most people cannot bear to listen to a phone ring without answering it. It's easy to not answer a letter, but it's hard to not answer a phone. Let me pass along a solution that has changed my life. When I was in the Nixon Administration, my telephone was tapped—I had been associating with known journalists. So I took an interest in the instrument itself. Turn it upside down; you will notice a lever that says "louder." Turn it away from the direction of louder. That is the direction of emancipation. If somebody needs to see you, he'll come over. If others need to tell you what they think, or even express how they feel, they can write. There are those who will call you a recluse—but it is better to listen to your own different drummer than to go through life with a ringing in your ears.

—WILLIAM SAFIRE

(*See Environment, Method.*)

WRITER'S BLOCK

There's absolutely no way to prevent an attack of "writer's fatigue." It's like the flu; when it hits, it hits . . . your concentration begins to flag, you lose your mental focus and for a moment can't remember what point you were trying to make. . . . Accept the attack for what it is, and take a break . . . put your writing project out of mind—read a spy novel, paint the garage, ride your bike, listen to music, go to a movie. Just remember that taking a break to clear the cobwebs out of your brain and to recharge your batteries is part and parcel of the writing process.

—HERBERT E. MEYER AND JILL M.
MEYER

268

Having to write about things other people tell you to write invariably leads to writer's block. If you concentrate on your own interests, you've licked most of the problem.

—KENNETH ATCHITY

Free write . . . write nonstop, continuously, never lifting the hand from the paper, putting down whatever thoughts occur, and when no thoughts come, filling in with repetition or nonsense. This method helps to break down that instant self-censorship which grips even very good students when they start to write.

—NANCY PACKER

You might enjoy Writer's Block as some people enjoy their illnesses, removing them from the responsibilities of running their lives. If you do love Writer's Block, and I think we all do sometimes, just as we like being laid up with the virus (under our covers where no one can touch us), remember this: The world feels sorry for you only for three days. After that, no one listens.

—LEONARD S. BERNSTEIN

When a writer is between books, he needs responsibility to keep him from making a fool of himself. Authors go through a period of craziness between books. Some invest in uranium stock, others change wives and agents. Some commit suicide. It's worse when you're young.

—JOSEPH HELLER

(*See Doggedness.*)

WRITING WORKSHOPS

People are always asking me if writing can be taught. My answer is, "No—I don't think writing can be taught." But on the other hand, if I were a young writer and convinced of my talent, I could do a lot worse than to attend a really good college workshop—for one reason only. Any writer, and especially the talented writer, needs an audience. The more immediate that audience is, the better for him because it stimulates him in his work; he gets a better view of himself and running criticism.

—TRUMAN CAPOTE

(*See Career Path.*)

BIBLIOGRAPHY

Writing Science Fiction and Fantasy, edited by Gardner Dozois, Tina Lee, Stanley Schmidt, Ian Randal Stock, and Sheila Williams, St. Martin's Press, 1991.

The Writer's Mind, Vol. II, edited by Irv Broughton, The University of Arkansas Press, 1990.

Writing the American Classics, edited by James Barbour and Tom Quirk, The University of North Carolina Press, 1990.

American Literary Anecdotes, by Robert Hendrickson, Facts on File, 1990.

World Literary Anecdotes, by Robert Hendrickson, Facts on File, 1990.

1990 Novel & Short Story Writer's Market, edited by Robin Gee, Writer's Digest Books, 1990.

Starting from Scratch, by Rita Mae Brown, Bantam Books, 1989.

Twelve Keys to Writing Books That Sell, by Kathleen Krull, Writer's Digest Books, 1989.

The Craft of Writing a Novel, by Phyllis Reynolds Naylor, The Writer Inc., 1989.

A Writer's Life, by Annie Dillard, Harper & Row, 1989.

On Being a Writer, edited by Bill Strickland, Writer's Digest Books, 1989.

The Writer's Chapbook, edited from *The Paris Review* interviews by George Plimpton, 1989.

The Art and Craft of Novel Writing, by Oakley Hall, Writer's Digest Books, 1989.

The Writer's Handbook, 1989 Edition, edited by Sylvia K. Burack, The Writer Inc., 1989.

How to Get Happily Published, by Judith Appelbaum and Nancy Evans, revised edition by Judith Appelbaum, New American Library, 1988.

Revising Fiction, by David Madden, Penguin Books USA, 1988.

The Modern World, Ten Great Writers, by Malcolm Bradbury, The Viking Press, 1988.

On Writing Well, by William Zinsser, third edition, Harper & Row, 1988.

The Bedford Reader, Third Edition, edited by X. J. Kennedy and Dorothy Kennedy, St. Martin's Press, 1988.

Writing Lives, Conversations Between Women Writers, edited by Mary Chamberlain, Virago Press, 1988.

The New Oxford Guide to Writing, by Thomas S. Kane, Oxford University Press, 1988.

How to Enjoy Writing, by Janet and Isaac Asimov, Walker & Co., 1987.

Visions & Voices, by Jonathan Cott, Doubleday & Co., 1987.

Getting Published, by Leonard S. Bernstein, William Morrow, 1986.

Writers on Writing, compiled by Jon Winokur, Running Press, 1986.

How to Write, by Herbert E. Meyer and Jill M. Meyer, Storm King Press, 1986.

Writer's Time, by Kenneth Atchity, W. W. Norton & Co., 1986.

The 29 Most Common Writing Mistakes and How to Avoid Them, by Judy Delton, Writer's Digest Books, 1985.

Novelists in Interview, John Haffenden, Methuen, 1985.

Simple & Direct, by Jacques Barzun, revised edition, Harper & Row, 1985.

Problem-solving Strategies for Writing, second edition, Harcourt Brace Jovanovich, 1985.

The Art of Fiction, by John Gardner, Alfred A. Knopf, 1984.

The Written Word, by Stephen White, Harper & Row, 1984.

On Becoming a Novelist, by John Gardner, Harper & Row, 1983.

On Native Grounds, by Alfred Kazin, Harcourt Brace Jovanovich, fortieth anniversary edition (1942), 1982.

The Writing Teacher's Sourcebook, by Gary Tate and Edward P. J. Corbett, Oxford University Press, 1981.

The Playboy Interview, edited by C. Barry Olson, Spencer Press, 1981.

The World Within the Word, essays by William H. Gass, Nonpareil Books, David R. Godine, Publisher, 1979.

The Reader Over Your Shoulder, Robert Graves and Alan Hodge, second edition, Random House (1943) 1979.

The Elements of Style, by William Strunk, Jr., and E. B. White, third edition, Macmillan, 1979.

The Author Speaks, Selected Publishers Weekly Interviews, 1967–1976, by *Publishers Weekly* editors and contributors, R. R. Bowker Co., 1977.

On Moral Fiction, by John Gardner, Basic Books, 1977.

Errors and Expectations, by Nina P. Shaughnessy, Oxford University Press, 1977.

The Norton Reader, fourth edition, W. W. Norton & Co., 1977.

Literary History of the United States, fourth edition, revised, Macmillan, 1975.

The Creative Writer's Handbook, Isabelle Ziegler, second edition, Harper & Row, 1975.

Popular Writing in America, by Donald McQuade and Robert Atwan, Oxford University Press, 1974.

On Writing, Editing and Publishing, by Jacques Barzun, second edition, The University of Chicago Press, 1971.

Structuring Your Novel, by Robert C. Meredith and John D. Fitzgerald, Harper & Row, 1971.

Ideas and Style, by Newman P. Birk and Genevieve B. Birk, The Odyssey Reader, Odyssey Press, 1968.

Tolstoy, by Henri Troyat, Doubleday, 1967.

Writers at Work, The Paris Review *Interviews,* third series, The Viking Press, 1967.

An Introduction to Literature, edited by Ralph H. Singleton and Stanton Millet, World Publishing Co., 1966.

The Art of Creative Writing, by Lajos Egri, The Citadel Press, 1965.

Writing Prose, edited by Thomas S. Kane and Leonard J. Peters, second edition, Oxford University Press, 1964.

Confessions of an Advertising Man, by David Ogilvy, Atheneum, 1963.

Writers at Work, Paris Review Interviews, Second Series, edited by Malcolm Cowley, Secker & Warburg, 1963.

Style, by F. L. Lucas, Collier Books, 1962.

Aspects of Fiction, by Howard E. Hugo, Little Brown & Co., 1962.

Wisdom for Our Time, edited by James Nelson, W. W. Norton & Co., 1961.

Writers on Writing, compiled and edited by Walter Allen, E. P. Dutton & Co., 1959.

Techniques of Fiction Writing, by Eloise Jarvis McGraw, The Writer Inc., 1959.

International Literary Annual, edited by John Wain, Criterion Books, 1959.

The Province of Prose, edited by William R. Keast and Robert E. Streeter, Harper & Bros., 1956.

A Treasury of the Essay, edited by Homer C. Combs, Spencer Press, 1955.

Fundamentals of Good Writing, by Cleanth Brooks and Robert Penn Warren, Harcourt Brace & Co., 1949.

The Art of Readable Writing, by Rudolph Flesch, Macmillan, 1949.

Understanding Fiction, Cleanth Brooks and Robert Penn Warren, F. S. Crofts & Co., 1948.

Story Writing, by Edith Ronald Mirrielees, The Viking Press, 1947.

The Writer's Handbook, edited by A. S. Burack, The Writer Inc., 1941.

The Summing Up, by W. Somerset Maugham, Doubleday, 1938.

The Enjoyment of Literature, by Elizabeth Drew, W. W. Norton & Co., 1935.

Becoming a Writer, by Dorothea Brande, J. P. Tarcher, Inc., 1934.

The Golden Book on Writing, by David Lambuth and others, Penguin Books, (first published 1923).

Quotation Books

The Almanac of Quotable Quotes from 1990, edited by Ron Pasquariello, Prentice Hall, 1991.

The Oxford Dictionary of Modern Quotations, edited by Tony Augarde, Oxford University Press, 1991.

A Dictionary of Literary Quotations, compiled by Meic Stephens, Routledge, 1990.

What a Piece of Work Is Man!, *Camp's Unfamiliar Quotations*, Wesley D. Camp, Prentice Hall, 1990.

Friendly Advice, compiled and edited by Jon Winokur, Dutton, 1990.

Handbook of Business Quotations, compiled by Charles Robert Lightfoot, Gulf Publishing Co., 1990.

The Macmillan Dictionary of Quotations, Macmillan Publishing Co., 1989.

The Concise Columbia Dictionary of Quotations, Robert Andrews, Columbia University Press, 1989.

The New Official Rules, by Paul Dickson, Addison-Wesley Publishing Co., 1989.

The Harper Book of American Quotations, Gordon Carruth and Eugene Ehrlich, Harper & Row, 1988.

Simpson's Contemporary Quotations, compiled by James B. Simpson, Houghton Mifflin Co., 1988.

The Speaker's Book of Quotations, compiled by Henry O. Dormann, Fawcett Columbine Books, 1987.

Barnes & Noble Book of Quotations, edited by Robert L. Fitzhenry, Barnes & Noble Books, a division of Harper & Row, 1987.

The New International Dictionary of Quotations, selected by Hugh Rawson and Margaret Minor, New American Library, a division of Penguin Books USA, 1986.

The Great Thoughts, compiled by George Seldes, Ballantine Books, 1985.

The Oxford Book of Aphorisms, chosen by John Gross, Oxford University Press, 1983.

Contradictory Quotations, Longman Publishers, 1983.

Familiar Quotations, John Bartlett (15th and 125th anniversary edition), edited by Emily Morison Beck and the editorial staff of Little, Brown & Co., 1980.

The Writer's Quotation Book, edited by James Charlton, Pushcart Press, 1980.

The Crown Treasury of Relevant Quotations, edited by Edward F. Murphy, Crown Publishers, Inc., 1978

The International Thesaurus of Quotations, compiled by Rhoda Thomas Tripp, Thomas Y. Crowell Publishers, 1970.

The International Dictionary of Thoughts, compiled by John P. Bradley, Leo F. Daniels, and Thomas C. Jones, J. G. Ferguson Publishing Co., 1969.

A New Dictionary of Quotations, selected and edited by H. L. Mencken, eighth printing, Alfred A. Knopf, (1942), 1966.

The Great Quotations, compiled by George Seldes, Lyle Stuart, 1960.

Best Quotes of '54, '55, '56, compiled by James B. Simpson, Thomas Y. Crowell Co., 1957.

The New Dictionary of Thoughts, originally compiled by Tryon Edwards, D. D., revised and enlarged by C. N. Catrevas, A. B., and Jonathan Edwards, Standard Book Co., 1956.

The American Treasury, selected, arranged, and edited by Clifton Fadiman, Harper & Bros., 1955.

Periodicals and Newspapers

Publishers Weekly   *The Wall Street Journal*
Writers Digest   *U.S. News & World Report*
The Writer
The New York Review of Books
The New York Times Book Review
The New York Times

INDEX